This
Weekend

Y. Olivo

The
EXPERIENCE
of CHRIST *as*
LIFE
for the
BUILDING UP
OF THE CHURCH

WITNESS LEE

Living Stream Ministry
Anaheim, California • www.lsm.org

First Edition, June 1994.

ISBN 0-87083-780-X

Published by

Living Stream Ministry
2431 W. La Palma Ave., Anaheim, CA 92801 U.S.A.
P. O. Box 2121, Anaheim, CA 92814 U.S.A.

Printed in the United States of America

01 02 03 04 05 / 11 10 9 8 7 6 5 4

CONTENTS

PREFACE

This book is composed of messages given by Brother Witness Lee in Los Angeles, California in the spring of 1969.

CHAPTER ONE

GROWTH IN LIFE BY THE FLOWING
OF THE TRIUNE GOD

Scripture Reading: Gen. 2:9; Psa. 36:9; John 1:4; 11:25; 14:6;
1 John 1:2; 5:12; Col. 3:4; John 4:10, 14; 7:38-39; Rom. 8:2, 6;
Rev. 22:1-2

The first point we want to cover in this book is how to
grow in life. The church life depends mainly on the growth
in life.

GOD, CHRIST, THE CHURCH, AND
THE LOCAL CHURCHES

In a sense, it is easy to know about God. Even the unbe-
lievers know about God. They know that there is an almighty
Being in this universe. But it is rather hard to know Christ.
In the first verse of the Bible in Genesis, God is revealed—"In
the beginning God created the heaven and the earth." The
first item revealed in the Bible is God.

Later, Christ is revealed in the Bible. The Gospel of John
says that in the beginning was God, the Word, and the Word
became flesh to dwell among us, full of grace and reality (1:1,
14). Christ is God plus something. The revelation in the Scriptures begins with God and goes on to Christ. Many human
beings know something of God. But only a small number of
people, relatively speaking, know Christ. Many Jewish people
know God, but they do not know Christ. We thank the Lord
that we Christians know not only God but also Christ.

All the real Christians know Christ, but very few know
the church. When we go on from the Gospels to Acts, there
is the church. Knowing the church is not as easy as knowing
Christ. After the church is revealed in the New Testament,

the local churches are revealed. In Genesis God is revealed; in the Gospels Christ is revealed; in Acts the church is revealed; and in Revelation the local churches are revealed. Thus, the Bible goes from God to Christ, from Christ to the church, and from the church to the local churches. The local churches are the last point of God's divine revelation. Revelation 1:11 says, "What you see write in a scroll and send it to the seven churches: to Ephesus and to Smyrna and to Pergamos and to Thyatira and to Sardis and to Philadelphia and to Laodicea." Here there are seven local churches in seven localities. I say again that this is the last point of the divine revelation in all the Scriptures.

Those Christians who are advanced know God, Christ, and the church. But thank the Lord that by His mercy, we know God, Christ, the church, and the local churches. We are not held in Genesis, the Gospels, or Acts. We are in Revelation! I like Genesis, but I do not want to stay there. I like the biography of the Lord Jesus in the four Gospels, but I do not want to stay there either. I like Acts, Romans, and Ephesians, but I do not want to remain in these books. I want to stay in the book of Revelation. Revelation will bring us into the New Jerusalem, which is revealed in its final chapters. Thus, we will never get out of the book of Revelation. We will be there for eternity.

We can get into the New Jerusalem through the local churches. In the first three chapters of Revelation, there are the local churches. Then in the last two chapters, there is the New Jerusalem. If you are in the local churches, there is no doubt that you will be in the New Jerusalem. We have to be in the beginning of the book of Revelation so that we can know the local churches.

A number of spiritual teachers know the church, but not the local churches. They talk much about the book of Ephesians, but they have not entered into the end of the divine revelation. The four main items revealed in God's divine revelation are God, Christ, the church, and the local churches. When we have the local churches, we have the church. Then we have Christ and God. This is because God is in Christ, Christ is in the church, and the reality and practicality of the church are in the local churches. If we want to find God, we must come to Christ. In order to find Christ, we must come to the church, and the reality and practicality of the church are in the local churches. Thus, if you are for the local churches, you are for everything. If you have the local church, you have the church; if you have the church, you have Christ; and if you have Christ, you have God. We all should declare, "Praise the Lord! I am in the local churches!"

In order to grow in life, we must know the local church. The local churches are the real expression of the church; the church is the real expression of Christ; and Christ is the real expression of God. In other words, God is expressed through Christ, Christ is expressed through the church, and the church is expressed through the local churches. People may talk about the universal church, but have they ever contacted it? What we can contact is the local church. Some might say that when we speak too much about the local church, we make the heavenly church earthly. But we must be clear that the local churches are the real expression of the heavenly church on the earth.

THE CHURCH BEING AN ORGANISM

We also need to see that the church is not an organization but an organism. But what is the difference between an organism and an organization? We can illustrate this by considering a chair and our physical body. A chair is an organization of lifeless material, but our physical body has life. Thus, it is an organism. Life makes our body an organism. The church is the Body of Christ, and as an organism it depends upon life. The church is an entity of life. It is produced by life and formed with life and in life. We have to see that the church is a life entity. It is not something formed by teaching or by organization. We cannot form, organize, or establish a church by our teachings, regardless of how spiritual they are. The church is born of life and formed of life. It is altogether an entity of life.

CHRIST AS LIFE TO BRING FORTH
THE BODY OF CHRIST

Now we need to ask, "What is life?" Christ is life. John 1:4

says that in Him is life. In John 11:25 and 14:6, He said that He is the life. Then the apostle Paul told us in Colossians 3:4 that Christ is our life. Christ is the life of the members of His Body. Who is Christ? Christ is God. Where is Christ? Christ is in the Spirit.

But this is still not fully clear. I want to give you a clear picture with a full scope of the matter of life from the entire Scriptures. God's intention in this universe is to bring forth the church as the Body of Christ. How could God produce such a Body? The first step He took was His creation. He created many things and eventually He created man in His own image (Gen. 1:26). But at the time of creation, God did not put Himself into man as life. He put man in the garden of Eden in front of the tree of life (2:9), and man at that time was an empty vessel.

Romans 9 tells us that we are vessels, containers (vv. 21, 23). Thus, man at the time of creation was in the image of God, but he was empty within. He was made as an empty vessel and put in front of the tree of life. God did this with the intention for man to partake of the tree of life, which signifies God Himself. Psalm 36:9 says that God is the fountain of life. Then John 1:4 says that in Him, the One who is the Word and God Himself, there is life. Life is in Him, so He is the tree of life.

The Lord is life, and we have to receive Him (John 1:12-13). If we have Him, we have life (1 John 5:11-12). The apostle John said, "And the life was manifested, and we have seen and testify and report to you the eternal life, which was with the Father and was manifested to us" (1 John 1:2). Christ is the life. When Christ was manifested, the life was manifested for us to receive. If you have the Son of God, you have life. By this life we have been regenerated, reborn, and by regeneration we have been produced as the members of the Body of Christ. Christ is the life of all the members of His Body, and eventually, this Body will be increased into the New Jerusalem.

In the New Jerusalem, we see the tree of life once again (Rev. 22:2). The tree of life in the garden of Eden was not within any human beings. It was standing there outside of man, and man was standing in front of the tree of life. But at the end of the divine revelation, the tree of life is within the New Jerusalem. This city is the composition of all the redeemed ones. This means that the tree of life will be within all the redeemed ones.

Furthermore, the tree of life in the New Jerusalem is growing in the river of life (vv. 1-2). Where the river of life flows, the tree of life grows. If the river of life is flowing in you, the tree of life is growing in you. When we have the flow of the river, we have the growing of the tree. This brief fellowship gives us a brief yet full picture of life in the entire Bible.

THE RIVER OF LIFE FLOWING OUT OF THE THRONE OF GOD AND OF THE LAMB

Revelation 22:1 says that the river of life flows out of the throne of God and of the Lamb. There is one throne, but how can two persons sit on one throne? You may say that the Bible tells us that Jesus is sitting at the right hand of God. So it must be that God is sitting at the left and Jesus is sitting at the right. But actually there is not one throne for two persons. Revelation 21 tells us that Christ is the lamp (v.23), and we know that God is the light (1 John 1:5). The light is within the lamp. On the throne there is not only God but also the Lamb. God as the light is within the Lamb as the lamp. He is the Lamb-God, which means that He is the redeeming God.

Genesis 1 does not say that in the beginning God and the Lamb created the heaven and the earth. It simply says, "In the beginning God...." But at the end of the Bible there are God and the Lamb. There is God plus something. In the beginning is God, but at the end is God plus the Lamb. Now He is not only God but also the Lamb-God.

Out of God who is in Christ, out of the redeeming God, flows the river of water of life. The river of life is simply the flowing of life, just as the current of electricity is the flowing of electricity. The river of life is life flowing. Thus, the river of life is God in Christ as the Spirit flowing. It is the flowing of God. Life is simply the Triune God flowing into us, through us, and out of us.

The pictures presented in the Bible, especially in Genesis

and Revelation, are very meaningful. Revelation shows us that God as the light is in the Lamb as the lamp. Out of the throne of the Lamb-God flows the river of life. This signifies that God in Christ as the Spirit—the Triune God—flows out to be received by us. We receive Him by drinking Him. When you drink of Him, He will flow into you. When you cooperate with Him some more, He will flow through you and out of you as the Spirit. John 7 tells us that what we drink and what flows out of us is the Spirit, who is God Himself (vv.37-39). Thus, life is God in three persons flowing into us, through us, and out of us.

HOW GOD FLOWS

Now we need to consider how God flows. The Bible shows us that God flows mainly in two steps. First, He flowed by being incarnated. He was in eternity in the heavens, dwelling in unapproachable light (1 Tim. 6:16), but one day He became incarnated. He came down to the earth to dwell among people. In this incarnated One, there was life and light.

Incarnation was the first step that God took to flow out. But this first step merely brought Him to the earth among people. He still could not get into us. Thus, He had to take a second step, the step of resurrection. The first step was incarnation, and the second step was resurrection. In order to be resurrected, He had to suffer death. By death He was brought into resurrection, and through resurrection He finished the second step of His flowing. By the first step, He was incarnated to be a man with the flesh. By the second step, He was transformed, changed in form, into the Spirit of life. In resurrection He is now the life-giving Spirit (1 Cor. 15:45b). Now He is not merely able to be on this earth among human beings, but He is also able to enter into us, His believers.

HOW TO ENJOY CHRIST AS LIFE

Now He is flowing in resurrection, and the way to receive Him is to drink Him in spirit by calling on His name—"O Lord Jesus, O Lord Jesus." The more you say, "Lord Jesus," the more you drink of Him. The more you say, "Lord Jesus," the more He flows in. He flows into us, through us, and out of us to water

the whole earth, to quench the thirst of all the ɪ
In the flow the tree of life grows, indicating tha
have this flow, you have the supply of life. The tree ᴏɪ ...
produces twelve fruits and yields its fruit each month (Rev.
22:2). The fruit is always new and fresh to meet every need.

In John 14:6 the Lord told us that He is the life. Then in
verses 7 through 11 He told us that He is one with the Father.
Philip said, "Lord, show us the Father and we will be satisfied." Then the Lord said, "I have been with you for so long a
time, and you do not know Me? Don't you know that I am the
Father? I am in the Father and the Father is in Me. I am one
with the Father. He who has seen Me has seen the Father."
Then in verses 16 through 20 the Lord told us that another
person would be sent—the Holy Spirit. As the Spirit, Christ
would come to enter into the disciples. Verses 7 through 11 tell
us that Christ is one with the Father. Verses 16 through 20
tell us that the Holy Spirit is the reality of Christ. Christ
is life to us by being the embodiment of the Father realized
as the Spirit. Romans 8:2 speaks of the Spirit of life, and
1 Corinthians 15:45b says that Christ as the last Adam
became a life-giving Spirit.

The key point to receiving Him and containing Him is our
human spirit. Romans 8:6 says that the mind set on the spirit
is life. If you want to receive the flowing Triune God as your
life, you have to open from the depths of your being to say, "O
Lord Jesus." If you want to enjoy Him as life all day long, you
need to call upon His name continually. The more you say,
"O Lord Jesus," the more you will enjoy Him. Do not try to be
humble or good. That does not work. Simply call upon the
name of the Lord.

How can you control your temper? When you feel like you
are going to lose your temper, simply say, "O Lord Jesus."
Then you will not lose your temper, but your temper will be
lost; in other words, it will go away. It will be lost by your
saying, "O Lord Jesus." Do not try to be humble or to love
others. The more you try to love someone, the more you will
not love him. Just call upon the Lord continually. Then everyone will be so lovable to you. This is the way to enjoy the
flowing of the Triune God as life.

Without the real experience of life, there is no practicality or actuality of the church life. Without the real experience of life, we will be divided. We do not need to talk about life in a doctrinal way. We need the real experience of life through the exercise of our spirit. We need to enjoy Christ by drinking Him and giving Him the free way to flow in us, through us, and out of us. Then we have the Father in the Son as the Spirit as our life. Daily and hourly we need to enjoy Him as our life. When we enjoy Him as life, we are humble and love others unconsciously. This life is nothing less than Christ Himself realized as the Spirit, who is flowing in our spirit. We need to exercise our spirit to say, "O Lord Jesus." Then we will enjoy the flowing of the living water in us, through us, and out of us. This is the way that we enjoy all the riches of Christ as the tree of life with the full, abundant, rich supply for the actuality of the church life.

CHAPTER TWO

GROWTH IN LIFE BY THE SOUL-LIFE BEING DEALT WITH

Scripture Reading: John 10:10; 3:5-6, 14-15, 29-30; 6:44-45; 7:17; 14:21, 23; 21:15-19; 12:25

THE LORD COMING THAT WE MAY HAVE LIFE FOR THE PRODUCING OF THE BRIDE

In John 10:10 the Lord said, "I have come that they may have life and may have it abundantly." We may know this verse and may even have some experience of it, but we need to ask, "Why did the Lord come that we may have life?" The Lord came that we may have life for the unique purpose that the bride might be produced.

We can prove this by John 3. In this chapter the words spoken by the Lord are short and simple, yet they are profound. The Lord came that we may have life, but how can we have this life? John 3 shows that we can have life by being regenerated, born again. It is through regeneration that we receive Christ as life. The way to be born again is to be born of water and the Spirit (v. 5). "Water" was the central concept of the ministry of John the Baptist, that is, to terminate people of the old creation. "Spirit" is the central concept of the ministry of Jesus, that is, to germinate people in the new creation. Water deals with all the negative things of our past, burying everything of our old history. Water buries the old life, and the Spirit brings in the new life.

The life which we have received by being born again is a life for us to enter into the kingdom of God (v. 3). Let me give an illustration to help us understand this. On the earth there are a number of kingdoms. There are the plant kingdom, the

animal kingdom, and the human kingdom. The only way to
enter into a particular kingdom is to have the life of that
kingdom. We entered the kingdom of humanity by being born
of human parents. Without having been born of human parents, we could never have seen, or entered into, the kingdom
of humanity.

In the universe there is another kingdom, the kingdom of
God. The only way that we can enter into this kingdom is by
being born of God. There is the kingdom of man, the kingdom
of humanity, and there is the kingdom of God, the kingdom of
divinity. We all have been born into the kingdom of humanity,
but we need to enter into the kingdom of divinity by being
born again of God. Nicodemus thought that to be born again
was for him to return to the womb of his mother (v. 4), but
to be born again is to be born of water and the Spirit. This
means to have our old history buried in the water and to have
a new beginning, a new life, a new history, a new day, a new
start of life, by the Holy Spirit. We have entered into the kingdom of God by a new birth, by regeneration, by being born of
water and the Spirit.

John 3 goes on to tell us that Jesus would be lifted up just
as the bronze serpent was lifted up by Moses in the wilder-
ness (v. 14). When He was lifted up on the cross, He was the
Lamb (1:29), but He was in the form of a serpent. In John 1 is
the Lamb, and in John 3 is the serpent. He was lifted up on
the cross as the Lamb of God to take away our sin, and He was
lifted up in the form of the serpent to deal with Satan, the old
serpent, so that we might have the divine, eternal life (v. 15).

Surely His being lifted up was also to accomplish redemption, but redemption is not the goal. Redemption is the
procedure for the goal. Redemption is for life. Through
redemption we receive life. Praise the Lord that today we are
not only redeemed but also born again. The past is gone and a
new life is now our portion. We have the eternal life, which is
God Himself flowing into us. Life is simply God Himself in
Christ as the Spirit flowing into us.

God has flowed Himself out and into us by two steps—by
incarnation and by resurrection. Incarnation accomplished
redemption, and resurrection imparts life into us. It was by

the step of incarnation that He became a man (John 1:14). As a man He was the Lamb of God lifted up on the cross in the form of a serpent to take away sin and to deal with Satan in His accomplishment of redemption. Then He was resurrected to become the life-giving Spirit (1 Cor. 15:45b). Christ as the Lamb of God is in chapter one of John. Christ as the breath, as the life-giving Spirit, is in chapter twenty. After He was resurrected, He came back to His disciples and breathed into them, telling them to receive the Holy Spirit (v. 22). When we believed into Him, we received Him by breathing Him in. Now we have Him within us as our life.

Eventually, in John 3:29 Christ is revealed as the Bride-groom who is for the bride. We are the bride. We might wonder how we fallen sinners could be a part of Christ's glorious bride. We become a part of this glorious bride by redemption and regeneration. John 3 shows us the start of life and the consequence of life. The start of life is to be regenerated by receiving redemption. The consequence of life is to enter into the kingdom and become a part of the bride. By being redeemed and regenerated we have entered into the kingdom of God and have become a part of the bride.

TRANSFORMATION BY DRINKING CHRIST, FEEDING ON HIM, ABIDING IN HIM, AND BREATHING HIM IN

After being regenerated, we need transformation. We can be transformed by drinking Christ, feeding on Him, abiding in Him, and breathing Him in all the time. John chapter four tells us how to drink of Him. Chapter six tells us how to feed on Him. Then chapters fourteen and fifteen tell us how to abide in Him. Finally, chapter twenty tells us how to breathe Him in. As we breathe Him in, we are refreshed. Christ is the real refreshment. We need to be refreshed by Christ day by day. By drinking, eating, abiding, and breathing, we grow in the divine life. If you are really drinking of Christ, feeding upon Him, abiding in Him, and breathing Him in day by day, you will have the growth.

DEALING WITH THE SOUL-LIFE

Now I want to point out another side of the growth in life.

Although we have been born of the Spirit, we still have the flesh with us. We have the flesh without and the Spirit within. To grow in life means to have the Spirit within you increasing all the time and the flesh without decreasing all the time. Colossians 3 says that in the new man, the Body of Christ, the church, there is no natural person (vv. 10-11). In other words, there is no American, Chinese, Canadian, Japanese, Mexican or any other race in the new man, but Christ is all and in all.

All of us in our flesh are like ugly worms, but within us there is something beautiful, which is the spiritual, heavenly, divine "butterfly." The Lord came that we might have life for the purpose of producing the Body, and in the Body there is nothing old. However, we are old in our natural man, so we need to be transformed. This is why we need to drink the Lord, eat the Lord, abide in the Lord, and breathe in the Lord all the time. But in order to be transformed, our soul-life must also be dealt with. Our mind, emotion, and will—our entire soul—must be dealt with by the Lord.

In John 6:44-45 the Lord said, "No one can come to Me unless the Father who sent Me draws him; and I will raise him up in the last day. It is written in the prophets, 'And they shall all be taught of God.' Every one who has heard and learned from the Father comes to Me." The Father draws us to His Son, the Lord Jesus Christ, by enlightening our mind. The real meaning of repentance is to have a change in your mind. Even today we still need some change in our mind. Our mind can frustrate us from coming to Christ. Day by day, morning and evening, we need a change of mind. We need the enlightenment of the Father so that we may realize our oldness. We need the renewing of our mind. Our mind needs to be taught by the Father afresh every morning.

We need the Father's teaching not man's teaching. The Father's teaching enlightens our mind that we may see the things in our concept and understanding that replace Christ. We might have something good in our mind which replaces Christ, so we need to repent. We need to have a change of mind, a change of our concept. Never be satisfied with what you understand. Never remain in your old concept. In John 5 the Lord told the Jewish people that they had the knowledge from the Old Testament, but they would not come to the Lord Jesus for life (vv. 39-40). We need to be enlightened and have our mind renewed again and again.

In John 6 there is the renewing of the mind. Then in John 7 there is the dealing with the will. The Lord Jesus said, "If anyone resolves to do His will, he will know..." (v. 17). This means that if we are going to know Christ and know the Father's intention, we must be submissive to take the Father's will. Then we will see that the Father's will is for us to enjoy His Son, the Lord Jesus Christ.

We may be exercising to drink the Lord, eat the Lord, abide in the Lord, and breathe in the Lord, but in many things we do not want to have a change of mind, and we do not want to have our will subdued to the Father's will. Thus, we may have the feeding, the eating, but not the proper digestion. You may exercise to enjoy the Lord, yet you are not willing to be enlightened in your mind and subdued in your will. As a result, it is difficult for you to partake of the Lord in a full way. Also, it is difficult for you to realize how much the Son of God means to you. The proper drinking and eating of the Lord must be realized in the change of the mind and in a submissive and subdued will.

The growth in life is Christ increasing within you and you decreasing all the time. If Christ is going to increase in you and you are going to decrease, you need a change of mind in your concept and you need a submissive will. The more we are changed in our mind and subdued in our will, the more Christ will be increased within us. This is the growth in life for the local church.

We can have the reality of the church life only by the growth in life. If we are short of the growth in life, we are short of the building up. The building up of the church life depends absolutely upon the growth in life. The real growth in life is not the increase of knowledge, of gifts, or of power. It is the increase of Christ within us. The increase of Christ within us requires that we have our mind changed and renewed and our will subdued.

John 14 shows that we need to have our emotion dealt

with. The Lord said, "He who loves Me will be loved by
My Father, and I will love him and will manifest Myself to
him....If anyone loves Me, he will keep My word, and My
Father will love him, and We will come to him and make an
abode with him" (vv. 21, 23). Love is with the emotion in the
heart. Thus, in John 6 the mind is enlightened, in chapter
seven the will is subdued, and in chapter fourteen the emotion is stirred up by the Lord. The real love of the Lord will
bring Him to you. If you love Him, He will manifest Himself
to you. If you love Him, He and the Father will come to you
and make a mutual abode with you. This is a matter of the
emotion. Our mind has to be renewed, our will has to be subdued, and our emotion has to be stirred up to love the Lord.

At the end of the Gospel of John, the Lord Jesus dealt with
Peter in a simple way. The resurrected, glorified Lord asked
him, "Simon, do you love Me?" When Peter said that he did,
the Lord said, "Feed My lambs" (21:15). When you love the
Lord, there is an outflow of life to feed others, to minister
Christ as life to others. We may say that we are enjoying
the Lord, but our mind has not been changed, our will has not
been subdued, and our emotion has not been touched by the
Lord or stirred up by Him. We surely need the drinking,
eating, abiding, and breathing, but we also need our soul
dealt with. The enjoyment of the Lord requires us to have a
change in our mind, to have our will subdued, and to have our
emotion stirred up to love the Lord.

The Lord Jesus went on to touch Peter's strong will, but
He did it in a wise way. He did not rebuke Peter and tell him
that his will was strong and stubborn and that some day
his will would be subdued. Instead the Lord said, "When
you were younger, you girded yourself and walked where you
wished; but when you grow old, you will stretch out your
hands, and another will gird you and carry you where you do
not wish to go" (v. 18). This shows the ripening of life, the
maturity in life, not merely the growth in life.

The more mature you become, the more submissive you
are. When you are young, you are stubborn in your will, and it
is so easy for you to debate and argue with others. But if you
are growing in the Lord, the day will come when you will

be very submissive. When you are ripe in the life of Christ, you will never argue with the brothers. You will go along with others. Even if they put you on the cross, you will say, "Amen." To go along with a fellow member needs the growth in life and the ripening in life, the maturity in life.

The Lord predicted that one day Peter would be a submissive person, not only submissive to God's will, God's hand, but also submissive to all of his environment without any resistance. If we have the maturity in life, we can say, "No matter what happens to me, no matter what betides, I will not resist." We need the mature ones in the church life. The young ones know how to fight, but they do not know how to be coordinated. To be coordinated requires a certain degree of maturity. If we have only life without growth, there will be fighting in the church life all the time. We need the growth in life for the maturity in life.

Peter was a bold and strong man, but the Lord told him that the day would come when someone would gird him and bring him to a place where he did not want to go, yet he would still go. Then the Lord said, "Follow Me" (21:19). If we love the Lord, that will afford us an outflow of life to minister life to others. But to be submissive in the will affords us the ability to follow the Lord. If we are going to follow Him, we need a real subduing of our will.

You need a submissive will, but it cannot come to you overnight. You need the growth in life, bit by bit, until you have the maturity in life. The local church is not only a place where you can receive life but also a place where you can grow in life to be matured in life. The real growth in life is, positively, the increase of Christ within you, and negatively, the decrease of yourself. This decrease is in the change of your mind, the subduing of your will, and the stirring up of your emotion.

In John 12:25 the Lord said, "He who loves his soul-life loses it; and he who hates his soul-life in this world shall keep it unto eternal life." We have to lose the soul-life, the psuche, to participate in the eternal life, the zoe. We lose the soul-life for the divine life. We have to lose the soul-life, the natural life, in three directions: in the change of the mind, in the subduing of the will, and in the stirring up of the emotion. Day by day we need the fresh renewing of our mind, the subduing of our will, and the stirring up of our emotion so that our emotion is on fire for the Lord. This needs to take place continually until we become a mature person in the divine life. The more you are matured, the more submissive you will be in your will to the Lord, to the environment, to the church, and to all the brothers and sisters around you. Then there will be no problems in the church life.

We have to grow in life by drinking the Lord, feeding on Him, abiding in Him, and breathing Him in. We also have to continually have a change of mind, have our will subdued, and have our emotion stirred up. The entire soul-life must be lost for the divine life. Then day by day the church life will be strengthened and built up.

CHAPTER THREE

THE CHURCH AND
THE LIFE FOR THE CHURCH

Scripture Reading: John 14:6-11, 16-20; 16:13-15; 1 Cor. 15:45b; 6:17; 2 Cor. 3:6b, 17; 13:14; 2 Tim. 4:22; Rev. 22:1-2

LIFE AND THE CHURCH

In this book our burden can be expressed with these two words—life and the church. If we are going to have a proper church life, we must pay adequate attention to the matter of life. The church is not something produced by doctrine or organization. The church is an organism, which is entirely a matter of life. Without life, there is no organism. The church is not only the house of God (1 Tim. 3:15) but also the Body of Christ (Eph. 1:22-23). For the church as the Body of Christ, we need life.

GOD'S INTENTION

God's intention seen throughout the Bible is that man would receive Him as life to become His expression in this universe. The first two chapters of the Bible and its last two chapters show us His intention in a particular way. These two sets of chapters are connected directly to each other.

In Genesis 1 and 2 we see God's creation. God created the heavens and the earth and many things for man to exist in this universe. Then God created man to fulfill His purpose. Man was created in the image of God (Gen. 1:26). The New Testament says that Christ is the image of the invisible God (Col. 1:15a). This means that man was created according to Christ. Just as a glove was made in the image of a hand in order to contain a hand, man was made in the image of Christ in order to contain Christ. God's intention is to put

Christ into man. A container is always made in the form, the style, and the image of its content. If a container is going to contain something round, it also must be round to match its content. A glove is made with five fingers because it contains a hand with five fingers. Likewise, man was made according to the image of Christ because God's intention was to put Christ into man.

But at the time of creation in Genesis 1, man was an empty container, an empty vessel. In Genesis 2 this empty vessel was put in front of the tree of life (v. 9). This, of course, was with the intention that man would partake of the tree of life to be filled with God as his content. Genesis 2 also tells us that there was a river flowing out of Eden to water the garden, and this one river was parted into four heads—one to the south, one to the north, one to the east, and one to the west—to cover the four directions of the populated earth (v. 10). No doubt, this river was the water for all the people on this earth. Thus, in Genesis 2 we see a tree of life with a flowing river. Then at the flow of this river there are three categories of precious materials—gold, bdellium (a pearl-like substance), and onyx stone (vv. 11-12). In the Bible, gold, pearl, and precious stones are for God's building.

In the last two chapters of the Bible, the tree of life appears again, and it appears in a river, the river of water of life (Rev. 22:1). This river is flowing in a city built of gold, pearls, and precious stones (21:18-21). The New Jerusalem is absolutely a city of gold. It has just one street, and the street of the city is also gold because it is a part of the city proper. The twelve gates are pearls, and the wall of the city is built with jasper stone. Twelve kinds of precious stones are the twelve layers of its foundation. Thus, gold, pearl, and precious stone seen in Genesis 2 are for God's building, which is consummated in Revelation 21 and 22.

We also need to see something more in Genesis 2. After the precious materials, there is a bride to be the increase of Adam. Adam was a bachelor, but after Eve came into being, Adam had a counterpart to match him. Adam is a type of Christ (Rom. 5:14), and Eve is a type of the church (Gen. 2:24; cf. Eph. 5:31-32). The church is the increase of Christ.

In order for Eve to come into being, God put Adam to sleep and took a bone, a rib, out of his side, with which He built a woman (Gen. 2:21-22). Sleep signifies death (1 Cor. 15:18; 1 Thes. 4:13-16; John 11:11-14). Christ was made to sleep, to die, on the cross, and His side was also opened up. Out of Christ's side flowed blood and water (John 19:34). Blood is for redemption, to deal with sin (1:29; Heb. 9:22). Water is for imparting life to deal with death (John 12:24; 3:14-15). The flowing water out of the Lord's side and the rib out of Adam's side both signify the resurrection life by which the church comes into being. The church is built and constituted with Christ as the resurrection life.

In the first two chapters of the Bible are the tree of life, the river, three kinds of precious material, and the bride. In the last two chapters of the Bible are again the tree of life, the river, three kinds of precious material, and the bride, who is composed of all the precious materials as a building. The two ends of the Bible are united to each other.

Right after Genesis 2 we see the serpent in Genesis 3. This old serpent is seen throughout the entire Bible and will do his subtle work to damage and frustrate the Lord's work until he is cast out in Revelation 20 (vv. 2-3, 10). The first two chapters of the Bible, before Satan came in, are continued by the last two chapters of the Bible, after Satan is cast out. Today we are in the experience of Revelation 12, where there is a struggling between the old serpent and the wife, the woman. I hope that not long from now we will enter into the day when Satan is cast out. Then we will enter into the last two chapters of the Bible.

HOW GOD ACCOMPLISHES HIS INTENTION

My intention in sharing this is that we would have a full scope of the revelation in God's writings. This full scope impresses into us that God's intention is to have a bride. God's intention is to have the Body, the church, as the counterpart of Christ. How can God accomplish His purpose? The first two chapters of the Bible show us how.

God put His created man in front of the tree of life. Actually, God is putting all of humanity in front of the tree of life. The tree of life is the Triune God, the incarnated God realized as the Spirit. God's intention is for men to open up their mouths to call on the Lord (Rom. 10:12-13). Then the tree of life will get into them. When you receive the Lord Jesus, you receive the tree of life. After the tree of life gets into you, there is a living river flowing within you and a spring of water within you gushing up all the time (John 4:14).

By this flowing of the living river, the precious materials will be produced. This means that by the tree of life with the flowing river, we men of clay, of dust, will be transformed into gold, pearls, and precious stones. We are the worthless dust, the clay, but we have some amount of gold within us. Praise the Lord that the gold within us is being increased all the time and the dust is being reduced. Regardless of how dusty we are, we all will eventually become gold, pearls, and precious stones.

These precious materials are not individualistic pieces. All of them are built up together into a corporate entity. At the end of Genesis 2, the rib is built into one bride. In Revelation 21 and 22 the gold, pearls, and precious stones are built together as one city, one bride, the consummation of the church. I hope we can see this picture from the Bible concerning how the church comes into being.

Many Christian leaders and teachers have a wrong concept. They think that the more doctrines they give people, the more the church will be built up, but this is not true. Actually, the more doctrines you give people, the more divisions and sects you will create. Doctrines divide. If you insist on your doctrine, and I insist on mine, we will be divided into two groups with two opinions. The church does not come into being by doctrines. The church comes out of life. It is a life entity. May the Lord have mercy on us. We must be brought into the full realization of life. The church can come into being only by life.

THE INNER FLOWING OF THE TRIUNE GOD
FOR THE CHURCH LIFE

Life is God Himself flowing out in Christ as the Spirit. He flows Himself into us as our life. Life is God Himself in His

Divine Trinity dispensing Himself into us in the person of the Father as the source, in the person of the Son as the course, and in the person of the Spirit as the flow. This is the way that He imparts and distributes Himself into us. To believe in the Lord Jesus is not just to be redeemed and forgiven. To believe in the Lord Jesus is to receive the Lord Jesus into you. He can come into you because today He is the life-giving Spirit (1 Cor. 15:45b).

All that the Father is and has is in the Son. The Lord Jesus said, "All that the Father has is Mine" (John 16:15a). He is the embodiment of the Father. God the Son put on human nature and was identified with us in incarnation. He was then crucified and resurrected to become the life-giving Spirit. In His ascension He obtained all the authority in heaven and on earth. He also obtained the highest name, the kingdom, the lordship, the kingship, and the headship over all things. He attained to the highest peak of the whole universe. He is far above all as the transcendent One above everything. All that the Father has is in Him, and in Him everything has been accomplished, obtained, and attained. Now all of this is in the all-inclusive Spirit.

Christ today is the life-giving Spirit. Second Corinthians 3:6 says that the letter kills, but the Spirit gives life. Verse 17 says that the Lord is the Spirit. In J. N. Darby's translation of the New Testament, he puts verses 7 through 16 of 2 Corinthians 3 in parentheses. This means that verse 17 is actually a direct continuation of verse 6. Therefore, Christ the Lord is the Spirit who gives life.

It is impossible for us to fully define the mystery of the Divine Trinity. John 1:1 says, "In the beginning was the Word, and the Word was with God, and the Word was God." It seems that the Word and God are two because the Word was with God, but the Word was God. Are They two or one? The first half of 2 Corinthians 3:17 says that the Lord is the Spirit, but the second half speaks of the Spirit of the Lord. Are They two or one? This is a mystery. We cannot fully understand the mystery of the Triune God, but we can receive Him and enjoy Him. Day by day we eat many things that we do not understand. But we can still receive them and enjoy them. The

Father in the Son as the Spirit flows into us as life for us to enjoy.

In John 14:6 the Lord said that He is the life and that no one can come to the Father except through Him. A number of Christians can quote this verse, but they do not pay adequate attention to the following verses. Verses 7 through 9 say, "If you had known Me, you would have known My Father also; and henceforth you know Him and have seen Him. Philip said to Him, Lord, show us the Father and it is sufficient for us. Jesus said to him, Have I been so long a time with you, and you have not known Me, Philip? He who has seen Me has seen the Father; how is it that you say, Show us the Father?"

Philip asked the Lord to show him the Father and then he would be satisfied. Then the Lord showed him that He was one with the Father and even was the Father, because when you saw Him, you saw the Father. The Lord went on to say, "Do you not believe that I am in the Father and the Father is in Me? The words that I say to you I do not speak from Myself, but the Father who abides in Me does His works" (v.10). When the Lord spoke, the Father was working. Isaiah 9:6 says that a son is given to us, but His name is called Eternal Father. All of this means that the Lord Jesus is not only the Son of God but also the Father.

In the following portion of John 14, the Lord went on to say that another Comforter would come to abide within the disciples. This chapter reveals that the second One, the Son, is one with the first One, the Father, and the third One, the Spirit, is one with the second One, the Son. In verse 17 the Lord said to the disciples that "He [the Spirit of reality] abides with you and shall be in you." Then in the next verse He said, "I will not leave you as orphans; I am coming to you." "He" and "I" are interchangeably used here. This means "He" is "I" and "I" is "He." In other words, the third One, the Spirit, is the second One, Christ. Christ who was in the flesh went through death and resurrection to become the life-giving Spirit.

The Lord said, "I am coming to you." This coming was fulfilled on the day of His resurrection. After His resurrection the Lord came back to His disciples to be with them forever, thus not leaving them as orphans. John 20 tells us how He came back to His disciples. The disciples were in a room with all the doors shut because they were afraid of the Jews. Suddenly Jesus appeared and stood in their midst (v. 19). He breathed into His disciples and said, "Receive the Holy Spirit" (v. 22). Then He disappeared from their physical sight, but He had entered into their spirit. The resurrected Jesus as the Spirit who gives life was in the spirit of all the disciples.

Thus, regardless of where the disciples went, He was with them. When Peter told the disciples that he was going fishing, going back to his old occupation, they followed him (John 21:3). The Lord also was with them because He had entered into their spirit. Today, of course, it is the same with us. If we go to the meeting, the Lord comes with us with joy. But if we go to the movies, He goes with us in sorrow. You can never get away from Jesus within you. Once He gets in you, you may want to divorce Him, but He will never divorce you. The Triune God has dispensed Himself as life into our spirit, and our spirit is now His dwelling place (Eph. 2:22).

In 2 Corinthians 13:14 Paul expressed his desire for the love of God, the grace of Christ, and the fellowship of the Holy Spirit to be with us all. These are three aspects of one thing. Love is the source, grace is the course, and fellowship is the flow. God the Father is in Christ the Son, Christ the Son is realized as God the Spirit, and God the Spirit is within us. Today this wonderful Triune God, who is ultimately and consummately the life-giving Spirit, is in our spirit. The Lord is within your spirit (2 Tim. 4:22).

At the conclusion of the Bible, we see that out of the throne of God and of the Lamb, the Lamb-God, the redeeming God, flows a river of water of life (Rev. 22:1). God the Father is within God the Son as the Lamb, and out of the throne of this Lamb-God flows God the Spirit as the river of water of life. This is a full picture of the Triune God flowing out and flowing into us as our life. By this flowing we are being transformed and built up. At the conclusion of the entire Bible, the river of water of life flows out of the Lamb-God throughout the entire city composed of all the Old Testament redeemed saints and all the New Testament believers. The twelve names of the twelve tribes on the twelve gates represent the Old Testament saints (Rev. 21:12), and the twelve names of the twelve apostles on the twelve foundations represent the New Testament believers (v. 14). Thus, the city is a composition of all the redeemed ones throughout all the generations. They are composed together as gold, pearls, and precious stones by the flowing of the living water.

Many of you have been faithful to the church life and are sincere to practice the church life. This is why I have the burden to share with you that the proper way to practice the church life is not by doctrines, forms, or gifts. It is by the flowing of the Triune God within us. The more He flows within us and through us, the more we will be transformed in our nature, our disposition, our very being, and the more we will be built up. This is the way to have the church life. Do not trust in doctrines or gifts. The Corinthian believers practiced the gifts, but the apostle Paul told them that they were fleshy. They spoke in tongues, but they were infants in Christ (1 Cor. 3:1). They were fleshy and soulish, so there were divisions among them (11:18-19). They did not have the building.

This shows that what we need is the flowing of the Triune God, the flowing of life. This is our burden. We should care only for the flowing of the inner life. This inner life is the Triune God as the Father who planned and purposed everything; as the Son who has accomplished everything, obtained everything, and attained to the highest place; and as the Spirit who is transmitting all that the Son is and has with the Father into us. It is a wrong concept to think that if we are properly instructed, corrected, and adjusted, we will be able to have the church life. This will not work. The only thing you and I need is the flowing of the inner life, the flowing of the Triune God.

This flowing of the living water within us is in our spirit. It is not in our mind, our opinions, our ideas, or our concepts. It is not in our emotion or will. It is absolutely, entirely, wholly, and fully in our spirit. The subtle enemy knows that this is the key point. This is why he tries to cover this matter and keep it hidden from the eyes of Christians. The human spirit, regenerated and indwelt by the Holy Spirit, is mentioned repeatedly throughout the Bible, but there is very little said about it today (see the book entitled Our Human Spirit published by Living Stream Ministry). Today the need is not for us to be taught, instructed, and corrected. The need today is for us to realize that the Triune God who planned and purposed in the Father and who accomplished what He purposed in the Son is now transmitting Himself into us as the Spirit to be our life. Now this Wonderful One in three persons is indwelling the deepest part of our being, that is, our human spirit.

By His flowing within our spirit, the church life comes into being. By His flowing within us, we are transformed day by day. We are not for outward instruction and correction. The inner flow of the Triune God takes care of everything. If you could be successful in adjusting yourself, you would become so proud. But it is not like this in the Christian life. Everything is carried out by the flow of the inner life. We should not be concerned so much about the saints' outward appearance or even their bad attitudes. Christ is the anointed One of God who is working within them to transform them. Instead of adjusting or correcting people, we need to bring them into the inner flowing of the Triune God.

The more the Triune God as the inner life flows within us, the more our whole being will be saturated with Him. By this life saturation little by little, day by day, and hour by hour, our mind is transformed, our will is subdued, and our emotions are purified. We are transformed by the inner flowing of the Triune God. How good it is to have the inner flowing!

CHAPTER FOUR

GOD'S GROWTH IN US FOR THE BUILDING

Scripture Reading: 1 Cor. 3:6-12; Eph. 2:21; 4:15-16; Col. 2:19; 1 Pet. 2:2-5

In the verses referred to in the Scripture reading there are two main concepts—the growth in life and the building up of the Body. First Corinthians 3 speaks of the planting, the watering, and the growing. Paul said that he planted; he sowed the seed. Then Apollos came to water, to irrigate. Then God gave the growth (v. 6).

We all need the planting of the life seed, not knowledge. The things of life are always in the Spirit. Knowledge is in the mind, but life is in the Spirit, and the Spirit is the reality of life. The Lord said, "It is the Spirit who gives life...the words which I have spoken to you are spirit and are life" (John 6:63). Romans 8:6 says that the mind set on the spirit is life. Life is in the Spirit, and knowledge is in the mind.

To plant is absolutely a matter of life in the Spirit, not a matter of mere teaching. This is why Paul told us that when he came to Corinth the first time, he did not use enticing words of man's wisdom, but he exercised his spirit to demonstrate the Spirit (1 Cor. 2:1-4). His speech was in demonstration of the Spirit, not of knowledge. By this he sowed the life seed, planting something of Christ into the spirits of the Corinthians. Then Apollos came to water the seed. God goes along with this organic work. When we plant and water, God follows to give the growth.

Paul told us that we are God's farm (3:9). Planting, watering, and growing are all for the farm, the cultivated land. On God's farm we have to grow something, and what we grow is Christ. Christ has been sown into us, and now Christ has to grow out of us. The Greek word for cultivated land in 1 Corinthians 3:9 means "farm" or "tilled ground." The church is God's farm to grow Christ.

Paul also said that we are God's building (v. 9). This indicates that the growth on God's farm is for the building. The church is built up by the growth in life. Whatever grows on God's farm is for the building. In other words, God's farm grows Christ, and Christ is for the building. The church is not built up by teaching or by organizing but by the growth in life. Paul planted, Apollos watered, and God gave the growth for the building up of the church.

CHRIST AS EVERYTHING TO US

First Corinthians is a precious book which follows the book of Romans in God's sovereign arrangement of the books of the Bible. Romans starts with the condemnation of sins and then goes on to justification, identification with Christ, the walk and life in the Spirit, and the Body life. But how can we have the Body life? For the answer, we need 1 Corinthians. If you want to have the Body life, you have to realize that Christ is everything to you. This is what 1 Corinthians reveals to us.

Chapter one tells us that we have been called into the fellowship, the participation, the enjoyment, of this wonderful One (v. 9). God has put us into Him (v. 30), and He is the power and wisdom of God (v. 24). Now we are in Christ, enjoying Him as everything. Chapter two tells us that if we are going to enjoy Christ, we have to give up our soul-life. Otherwise, we will be a soulish person, who always considers the things of Christ to be foolishness (v. 14). We have to be a person in the spirit so that we can enjoy this wonderful One. For our past Christ is our righteousness; for our present He is our sanctification; and for our future destiny He is our redemption (1:30). He is everything to us.

But if we are going to realize such a Christ, we have to be in the spirit. We may use electricity as an illustration of this. The electricity installed in a building can be applied only by turning on the switch. In the same way, Christ can be applied to us only by the exercise of our spirit. We have to be in the spirit. Then we will become spiritual persons (2:15; 3:1). A spiritual person is a person living, moving, acting, and having his being in the spirit.

TRANSFORMED INTO PRECIOUS MATERIAL FOR GOD'S BUILDING

First Corinthians goes on to tell us that something of Christ has been planted into us. The real ministry of life is like the ministry of Apollos, who watered the seed. God goes along with this watering and gives the growth. Christ has been sown into us, and Christ is going to grow out of us. When Christ grows out of us, this growth transforms us to produce the gold, silver, and precious stones (v. 12). According to our natural being, we are wood, grass, and stubble, but we are being transformed into precious material for God's building.

The Lord will not use anything of our natural being for His building. Some of the saints may be good in a natural way without any transformation in their nature or disposition. Our natural goodness has nothing to do with God's building. We were born as wood, grass, and stubble—worthless material for God's building. But we were reborn with gold, and we are being transformed into silver and precious stones by being watered and by our growth in life. We need the watering for the growth in life that we may be transformed. Thus, 1 Corinthians 3 shows us the planting, watering, growing, transforming, and the producing of precious material for God's building.

GOD'S BUILDING BY THE GROWTH IN LIFE

In this building no human hand can avail, because this growth is not in our hand. Paul said that both he who plants and he who waters are nothing (v. 7). Paul and Apollos are nothing. What counts is God Himself who gives the growth. We cannot do anything with our human hand. We cannot organize a church, but we can plant and water so that God can go along with our ministry to give the growth in life. Then something of Christ will grow up within others to transform them into precious material for God's building. This is

absolutely not something organized by the human hand but
something of the growth in life by God's life-giving power.

Ephesians 2:21 says that all the building is growing into a
holy temple in the Lord. If there is no growth, there is no
building. The building grows into a temple. We cannot organize something to be the house of God. The house of God is
something that grows up. Ephesians 4 says that we need to
hold Christ as the reality that we may grow up in all things
into Christ as the Head (v. 15). First, we grow into Christ.
Then all the Body receives something of Christ to minister to
the members. By this kind of ministry, the Body is built up by
growing (v. 16). Again we see the growth and the building.

GROWING WITH THE GROWTH OF GOD

Colossians 2:19 says that the real building of the Body
depends on the growth, and this growth comes from the
growth of God. God is eternally perfect and complete, but
this verse says that God grows. God in Himself needs no
growth, but in us He needs the growth. God is complete in
Himself, but He is not complete in us. The growth of the
Body of Christ has nothing to do with the doctrinal knowledge of the Bible, the way of worship, or any such matter.
Rather, the growth of the Body depends on the growth of God,
the increase of God's element, in the Body. We need the
growth of God within us.

God has to be added into our being again and again. This
is why we are told that we need to be filled unto all the fullness of God (Eph. 3:19). We have a little bit of God within us,
but we need more of Him added to us. When we are filled
with God, we will be "crazy" to speak about Christ. When
Paul was defending himself before King Agrippa, the Roman
politician Festus exclaimed, "You are insane, Paul. Much
learning is driving you insane" (Acts 26:24). Then Paul said,
"I am not insane, most excellent Festus, but I am uttering
words of truth and soberness" (v. 25). Actually Paul was crazy
for Christ because he was filled with God. If you are filled
unto the fullness of God, you will speak about Christ all the
time. We need to be filled with God for the growth of God. God
has to increase within us day by day. We grow not by the

increase of gifts, the increase of knowledge, or the increase of moral or ethical attainment. We grow only by the increase of God.

Let us consider two brothers. One brother is always adjusting himself to fit into certain situations. He is always nice and willing to be adjusted. We may mistakenly think that this is a very good brother who is full of life. Another brother is rough and tough. He is not very willing to be adjusted. But at times he is touched by the life-giving Spirit. You can realize that even though he is rough, there is the increase of God within him. This is the growth in life. If you would prefer the brother who is outwardly nice instead of the other brother who is inwardly experiencing the increase of God, this shows that you do not know what life is.

If we were asked to choose between Jacob and Esau, many of us would prefer Esau. Jacob was a supplanter, a heel holder, who was skilled at cheating others. He did not cheat others to their face but at their "heels." Jacob was someone who would cheat you behind your back. It seems that God was not fair to choose Jacob over Esau. God said that He loved Jacob and hated Esau (Rom. 9:13). Because Jacob cheated his brother Esau, he was forced to leave his home and go to his uncle Laban. While he was on his journey, he was forced to sleep in the open air, and he had a wonderful dream. When he awoke from that dream, he declared that the place where he slept was Bethel, the house of God. He set up the stone, upon which he had laid his head, as a pillar and poured oil upon it (Gen. 28:10-22). God's hand was upon him, not to do some outward correcting or adjusting work but to do an inner transforming work. God eventually told him that he would no longer be called Jacob but Israel (32:28). He would no longer be a supplanter but a prince of God.

What are we doing here in the church? Are we correcting, adjusting, and improving people? If we are doing this, we are in religion. It is the work of Confucius to improve people. Instead, we are here planting and watering that God may follow to give the growth so that people can be transformed into precious material for God's building. To grow and be transformed is to have God increasing in you all the time.

ALLOWING THE LORD TO TAKE OVER
OUR MIND, EMOTION, AND WILL

Previously, we were made clear about the dispensing of the Triune God. God the Father is the source. Whatever He is, is in the Son. The Son has accomplished all that the Father planned and purposed. He has attained the throne, the lordship, the kingship, the headship, the kingdom, and the highest name. All authority in heaven and on earth has been given to Him. Now all that the Son has accomplished, obtained, and attained with all that the Father is and has, is in the life-giving Spirit who has been dispensed into our spirit. We are one spirit with Him. The Triune God has been dispensed into our spirit. This is marvelously wonderful!

Our spirit is the central part of our being. Surrounding our spirit are the inward parts of the soul—the mind, emotion, and will. You have God in your spirit, but you do not have God in your mind, emotion, and will. You need to allow Him to dispense Himself into all the parts of your soul. Let us again use the illustration of electricity installed in a building. The only way to appropriate and apply this electricity is to turn on the switch. Our spirit is the switch that turns on and applies the heavenly electricity. We have to exercise our spirit so that God may saturate and take over our mind, our will, and our emotion. This is the growth in life. We have to turn to our spirit to meet God there.

In particular, we need to allow the Lord to subdue our will from within our spirit. We should pray, "Lord, I am willing to give You the ground. Take full possession of my will and saturate my will with Yourself." Then God will be increased within us, and we will have the growth of God in us. Many times we will not give the Lord the ground in our will in certain things. We may say that we have consecrated ourselves to the Lord and to the church. But even today we still would not be willing to surrender all the ground in our being to the Lord. Instead, we should say, "Lord, this is Your ground. Take it. I surrender in my will. I am willing to be subdued by You. Take over my will." Right away we will have the increase of God.

Our mind must also be possessed by the Lord. It is wrong

that we are in the mind daily. As those who are seeking the Lord, we must exercise to be in the spirit all the time. Two brothers coordinating together in the church service may realize that they have to be in the spirit, but they are used to being in their mind. One brother may consider in his mind about the other brother, thinking that this brother's attitude toward him has not been good. When we are in the mind, we are soulish and dusty. The more we think about the brothers apart from the spirit, the more dusty we become, to be the food of the serpent, who was assigned by the Lord to eat dust all the days of his life (Gen. 3:14).

When we are in the spirit, we will forget about everything but Christ. We must ask the Lord to be merciful to us so that we may surrender our mind to Him. We should say, "Lord, take over my mind. I give all the ground in my mind to You." Then God will increase in us more. We also need to give Him the ground to take over our emotion so that our emotion can be filled with His desires and feelings.

It is in this way that God is increasing within us all the time to cause us to grow with the increase of God. We do not grow by being outwardly adjusted, improved, or corrected. We grow by giving the Lord the ground within us so that He can increase within us. This issues in the transformation in life. By the growth in life we are transformed into precious stones for God's building. We become the living stones built up as a spiritual house (1 Pet. 2:5). The growth in life is a matter of God increasing in our whole being, beginning from our spirit and spreading into all of the inward parts of our soul. The more ground He gains within us, the more He increases Himself within us. Then we grow by His increase within us for the building up of the Body of Christ. This is the way to have the local church life.

CHAPTER FIVE

BEING SPIRITUAL FOR THE CHURCH

Scripture Reading: 1 Cor. 1:2, 10-13; 2:14-16; 3:1-4, 16, 21-23; 6:13b, 15a, 17, 19-20; 12:12; 14:5, 12, 37; 16:18

SPECIAL ITEMS IN FIRST CORINTHIANS

Christ as God's Power and Wisdom

In 1 Corinthians there are many special things which cannot be found in other books of the Bible. Chapter one tells us that Christ is the power of God and the wisdom of God (vv. 24, 30). Wisdom is for planning, purposing; power is for carrying out, accomplishing, what is planned and purposed. A rich person's capital is his power. But even if you are rich, powerful, you still need the wisdom to carry out things with your riches. If a car does not have gasoline, it does not have the power. But if a person does not have the adequate wisdom, he cannot drive the car. Both power and wisdom are needed to drive the car. In God's economy Christ is God's power and wisdom.

Christ as Our Righteousness, Sanctification, and Redemption

In the wisdom of God, three main things are included: righteousness, sanctification, and redemption (v. 30). Righteousness is for our past. Our past was a mess, but Christ is our righteousness for our past. Sanctification is for our present. We have to be holy, sanctified, but not by ourselves. Christ Himself is our sanctification. He is our sanctifying life for the present. In the future He will be our redemption for the redemption of our body.

The Lord of Glory, the Depths of God, and the Mind of Christ

In chapter two there are many wonderful items. Here Paul speaks of the mystery of God and of the things God fore-ordained and prepared for us which no eye has ever seen, no ear has ever heard, and which have not come up in man's heart (v. 9). But God has revealed them to us through the Spirit, and they have been graciously given to us by God (vv. 10-12). God has foreordained, prepared, revealed, and given Christ to us as the Lord of glory (vv. 7-8) and the depths of God (v. 10). First Corinthians 2 also says that we have the mind of Christ (v. 16).

I hope that we would remember five items in chapter one: power, wisdom, righteousness, sanctification, and redemption. All of these items are Christ Himself given to us as our divine portion from God. In chapter two we have to remember three things: the Lord of glory (v. 8), the depths of God, and the mind of Christ.

Planting, Watering, Growing, Transforming, and Building

In 1 Corinthians 3 we have seen the planting, watering, growing, transforming, and building (vv. 6-14). We are God's farm and God's building, and we are growing in life on God's farm to be produced as precious material for God's building.

The Temple of God

In chapter three Paul also speaks of the temple of God (vv. 16-17). The temple here is collective and corporate, not individual. We are many, but the temple is one. We can be made one by being fed, watered, built up, and transformed. By growing and being transformed we become the gold, silver, and precious stones, and we are built up together to be the temple of God. We are the temple of God, and the Holy Spirit dwells in us.

All Things Being for the Church

At the end of chapter three, Paul said, "All things are

yours, whether Paul or Apollos or Cephas or the world or life or death or things present or things to come; all are yours, but you are Christ's, and Christ is God's" (vv. 21-23). We need to realize that all things are for us, so all things are for the temple, the church. All things, including the heavens and the earth with all the plants, animals, and human beings, are for the church. Even Satan and the demons are for the church. Surely we hate Satan and the demons, but in His sovereignty God uses even them for the building up of the church.

Things present, things to come, life, and even death are for the church. All things are for the church. This is the fundamental point of God's purpose. God created the heavens, the earth, the angels, and all human beings for the church. God even allowed one of the angels to become His adversary, Satan, for the church. God also allowed many of the angels to rebel for the church. Everything is for the church.

The Corinthian believers foolishly said that they were of Paul and of Apollos, but Paul said that both he and Apollos were theirs. The church is not for Paul; Paul is for the church. Everything and everyone is for the church. All things are yours, and you are Christ's, and Christ is God's. This means that all things are for the church, the church is for Christ, and Christ is for God. All the fullness of the Godhead dwells in Christ (Col. 2:9), Christ is in the church, and the church is the center of the whole universe.

The Begetting Father

Now let us consider chapter four of 1 Corinthians. In verse 15 Paul said, "For though you have ten thousand guides in Christ, yet you do not have many fathers; for in Christ Jesus I have begotten you through the gospel." The Corinthians were not Paul's students; they were his children. He was their begetting father.

Absent in the Body, yet Present in the Spirit

In chapter five there is one striking point. Paul told us here that he could be far away from Corinth yet still attend the meeting there in his spirit. Verse 4 says, "In the name of our Lord Jesus, when you and my spirit have been assembled, with the power of our Lord Jesus." Paul said that when they met, he was there in his spirit. This shows that we can be far away from a place, yet still be there in our spirit. Paul not only attended their meeting but also exercised the Lord's authority to deliver a sinful one to Satan (v. 5). The apostle's spirit was so strong that his spirit was assembled with them to carry out his judgment upon an evil person.

One Spirit with the Lord

Now we come to chapter six. Verse 17 says, "He who is joined to the Lord is one spirit." This is a marvelous verse showing the believers' organic union with the Lord through believing into Him (John 3:15-16).

Our Body Being for the Lord and the Lord Being for Our Body

First Corinthians 6 also tells us that our physical body is for the Lord and the Lord is for our physical body (v. 13). Do you have some trouble in your body? If so, you should pray, "Lord, my body is for You, and You are for my body. You have to take care of my body." Chapter six is very deep. It reveals that not only our spirit but also our body is the dwelling place of God. Our body is a temple of the Holy Spirit (v. 19).

This corresponds with Romans 12, which says that if we are going to have the Body life, the church life, we must present our physical body to the Lord (v. 1). We may say that we love the Lord with our heart and serve the Lord in our spirit, but what about our body? We cannot say that we love the Lord and leave our body at home away from the church meetings. We also should have the realization that our body is for the church in the way that we dress. If we realized that our body is for the church, the Body of Christ, we would say, "Lord, how can I misuse my body? How can I usurp my body for other purposes? My body must be solely for Your Body. My body should not be an advertisement of the flesh or of the world. My body should be an advertisement of the Lord's Body."

We need to remember these three points: 1) he who is

joined to the Lord is one spirit; 2) our body is for the Lord and the Lord is for our body; 3) when we use our body properly, we have the Body life. If we misuse our body, the Body of Christ cannot be among us.

The Highest Point of Spirituality

Now let us consider 1 Corinthians 7. Paul told us here that he did not have the commandment of the Lord, but he expressed his opinion (v. 25). Whatever he expressed as his opinion, we have to take as the word of God. He expressed his opinion but he also said, "I think that I also have the Spirit of God" (v. 40). When we feel that we do not have the Lord's commandment, yet we express our opinion and this is of the Lord, this is the highest point of spirituality.

The Believers' Conscience

Chapter eight speaks about the believers' conscience. Paul speaks here of taking care of the weak ones and not wounding their weak conscience (vv. 11-12). The conscience is the main part of our spirit (Rom. 8:16; cf. 9:1). Whenever the conscience is damaged, the flow, the fellowship, of the Spirit is cut off. In other books the conscience is covered, but not in the way that Paul covers it in 1 Corinthians 8. This is because 1 Corinthians reveals that Christ is the life-giving Spirit indwelling our spirit (15:45b; 6:17), and the main part of our spirit is the conscience. If our conscience is damaged, the flow between us and the Triune God will be cut off. There will be insulation between us and the Lord, and we will feel deadened.

Sowing Spiritual Things and Enjoying Christ as Our Spiritual Food, Spiritual Drink, and Spiritual Rock

In chapter nine Paul said that he sowed spiritual things to the Corinthians (v. 11). Then in chapter ten he spoke of Christ as our spiritual food, spiritual drink, and spiritual rock (vv. 3-4).

Head Covering and the Lord's Table

Chapter eleven covers the truth concerning head covering (vv. 2-16) and the Lord's table (vv. 17-34). Head covering is related to the headship of Christ, and the Lord's table is related to the Body of Christ. Thus, chapter eleven takes care of the Head and the Body. It also speaks of the saints coming together not for profit but for loss (v. 17). Christians always think that as long as they come together that is good. But Paul said that we may come together not for the better but for the worse.

The Body Being Christ

The main point in chapter twelve is that the Body, the church, is Christ. Verse 12 says, "For even as the body is one and has many members, yet all the members of the body, being many, are one body, so also is the Christ." This verse is unique in the Bible, telling us that Christ is not only the Head but also the Body.

Christ as Love

Chapter thirteen shows us Christ as love. Tongues will cease, prophecies and knowledge will be rendered useless, but Christ as love never falls away (v. 8). He never fails, fades out, or comes to an end.

Prophesying Builds Up the Church

The main thing that chapter fourteen reveals is that prophesying builds up the church (v. 4b).

No Legality in the Church Life

In verse 31 Paul said, "You can all prophesy one by one that all may learn and all may be encouraged." But in 12:29 Paul said, "Are all prophets?" Thus, chapter twelve indicates that we are not all prophets, but chapter fourteen says that we can all prophesy. Also, chapter eleven says that women can pray and prophesy (v. 5), but chapter fourteen says that the women have to be silent (v. 34). These varying portions of the Word show that we should not be legal. Today is the age of the Spirit. We should not make any practice a legality. In his preface to The Normal Christian Church Life, Brother Watchman Nee said that he was afraid that people would take his book as a manual to make something legal.

Today is not the age of the law. In the law everything is mentioned clearly and definitely with no room for discussion. But in 1 Corinthians 11:34 Paul said, "The rest I will set in order when I come." This indicates that the apostle did not give instructions for everything related to the practice of the church. For "the rest" we need to seek the Lord's leading, based on and governed by the principles set forth in the New Testament. Paul spoke to the Corinthians about division in chapters one and three, about a sinful brother in chapter five, about a lawsuit in chapter six, about idol worship in chapter eight, and about head covering and the Lord's table in chapter eleven. But Paul did not tell them everything. If the apostle Paul could not come to us, what should we do? Paul cannot come, but the Lord is here.

If some say that we all have to pray-read, they have made pray-reading a legality. If others say that we should not pray-read, they have made this a legality. Nothing is right as long as it is a legality. When anything becomes a legality, that brings in death. We should say, "Lord, we thank You that You have not told us everything. We thank You that we have to open to You all the time." Should we have a piano or an organ? Should we have a hymnal? We should not make anything a legality. May the Lord be merciful to us that we would never be legal. If we are legal with anything, we are finished.

In 1 Timothy 2 Paul told the sisters that they should dress in modest apparel (v. 9). We cannot define the standard of modesty. How modest is modest? Who can make the decision to set the standard? On the one hand, the revelation of the Bible is complete. On the other hand, we need the living Spirit to guide us into the reality of all things. With the law there was no room for debate. But in the New Testament many details are left up to the inner leading of the Spirit. Of course, things concerning idol worship, heresy, and immorality are not debatable, but things concerning forms and practices should not be legal.

How long should our meetings be and at what time should they be? The Bible does not tell us these things. Then what should we do? This is why Paul said, "The rest I will set in order when I come." With so many questions and problems, we have to look to the Lord's presence. We should say, "Lord, we cannot find any regulation in Your Word, but You are the living Word." We need a living contact with the Lord. We have to take all the regulations and instructions of the New Testament in spirit. The letter of the Old Testament and of the New Testament is killing. It is the Spirit who gives life (2 Cor. 3:6).

The Last Adam Becoming a Life-giving Spirit

Paul goes on in 1 Corinthians 15 to say that the last Adam became a life-giving Spirit (v. 45b). In incarnation Christ became flesh for redemption (John 1:14, 29). Then in resurrection He became a life-giving Spirit for the impartation of life (John 10:10b).

Being Refreshed in Our Spirit

In 1 Corinthians 16 Paul pointed out that certain faithful ones refreshed both his spirit and the spirits of all the saints (vv. 17-18). Paul did not say that they refreshed his mind, emotion, or loving heart. He said that they refreshed his spirit. You cannot find this point anywhere else in the Bible. This is because in this book the apostle's intention is to tell us that we have to always be in the spirit. If we are not in the spirit, it is impossible for us to experience Christ and have the church life.

In 1 Corinthians Paul did not say as much about himself as he did in 2 Corinthians. Brother Watchman Nee said that 2 Corinthians may be considered as an autobiography of Paul. But still in his first Epistle you can see that he is a person behaving, acting, working, moving, and having his being in the spirit. Chapters four, five, and seven show that Paul was such a person, a person absolutely in the spirit. Then in the last chapter he said the brothers who came to him refreshed his spirit. Paul cared for his spirit first. He was a person altogether in the spirit.

A BOOK FOR THE CHURCH

We have to remember that 1 Corinthians is not a book for the individual believers, but a book for the church. We have to pay attention to the second verse of this book, in which Paul addresses the church of God in Corinth with all those who call upon the name of the Lord Jesus Christ in every place. It is not and but with all those who call upon the Lord's name. If Paul had used the word and, that would mean that all the saints were standing on the same level as the church. But Paul used the word with, indicating that the saints belong to the church. If we say, "The parents came with the children," this means that the children belong to the parents. This book was written to the church with all the saints. This means that all the saints need a church with which they can be identified.

This book is full of a church concept. All that was written in it is with a church-consciousness. It was not a book written to an individual, but to the local church with all the saints. If we want to know this book, we have to be in the church. If we are not in a local church, we do not have the proper standing, qualification, or position to understand it. If we want to see a particular thing, we have to be positioned at the proper angle, and the proper angle for us to understand this book is the local church.

HAVING THE SAME MIND AND OPINION AND SPEAKING THE SAME THING

In 1:10 Paul said, "Now I beseech you, brothers, through the name of our Lord Jesus Christ, that you all speak the same thing and that there be no divisions among you, but that you be attuned in the same mind and in the same opinion." It is possible to have the same mind and opinion and speak the same thing only when we are in the spirit. When we are in the soul, we can never have the same mind. The only way is for us to be transformed by remaining in the spirit.

In verse 13 Paul said, "Is Christ divided?" Paul said this because Christ is in you, in me, and in all the saints. This implies that we have to forget about ourselves and simply take Christ. Then we are one. If we do not take Christ practically in our daily life, how can we be one with one another? It is impossible. We are many individuals, but Christ is one. When we are in ourselves, we are many, but when we have Christ and are in Christ, we are one.

OUR NEED TO BE SPIRITUAL MEN
FOR THE CHURCH LIFE

In chapter two Paul reveals that to have Christ, to realize Christ, to experience Christ, and to partake of Christ, we need to be spiritual not soulish. The soulish man, the man in the soul, can never realize the things of Christ (v. 14). This is like trying to realize sound with your eyes. Sound can be realized only by our hearing organ. Christ is the life-giving Spirit and He can be realized only by our spiritual organ, that is, our spirit. Only the spiritual man can discern the depths of God, which is Christ Himself (vv. 10-11, 15).

This is not just a doctrine. We have to be in the spirit so that the Spirit can saturate our soul and take over our whole being. Then we can say, as Paul said in 2:16, that we have the mind of Christ. We in this verse does not refer to the fleshly or soulish believers at Corinth but to the ones in verse 6 who preach God's wisdom and minister the spiritual things to the spiritual persons (v. 13). These are the apostles and all those who walk in the spirit. The fleshly and soulish believers cannot say that they have the mind of Christ.

Romans 12:2 tells us to be transformed by the renewing of the mind. Only the regenerated and transformed Christians can say that they have the mind of Christ. A person like Paul is qualified to say that he has the mind of Christ because he is spiritual and he has been transformed by having his mind renewed with the saturation of the Holy Spirit. Such a person can express his opinion because he has the mind of Christ. His opinion has something of Christ.

A soulish man is a natural man, one who allows his soul (including the mind, the emotion, and the will) to dominate his entire being and who lives by his soul, ignoring his spirit, not using his spirit, and even behaving as if he did not have a spirit (Jude 19). Soulish Christians like to argue and debate over doctrinal matters.

Some Christians are even worse than soulish. Paul said that the Corinthian believers were fleshly and even fleshy (3:3, 1). This means that they were totally of the flesh. First Corinthians 5 and 6 describe what it is to be fleshy. There are the immoral things such as fornication and adultery in chapter five and contentions, envying, and strife leading to lawsuits among the believers in chapter six.

Paul, of course, was neither fleshy nor soulish. He was a spiritual man. Paul demonstrated the Spirit by exercising his spirit (2:4). His spirit was so strong that he attended the Corinthians' meeting in his spirit even though he could not be there physically. With fleshly and soulish people, there is no possibility of having the church life. Only spiritual people can have the church life.

Today there is a wrong concept among seeking Christians. The fundamental Christians think that the church can be built up by teachings. The Pentecostal Christians think that the church can be built up by the gifts. But history has shown that doctrines and gifts have divided the Lord's children. The only way that the church can be built up is for us to be spiritual Christians, Christians who live according to our spirit mingled with the Spirit of God.

We should care only for the enjoyment of the Lord. Then we will be of one mind, of one opinion, and we will speak the same thing. When we turn to our spirit, we are the same. As we live in the spirit, the church as the farm of God will grow Christ. Christ has been sown into us, and now He needs to grow out of us. What we need today is to turn ourselves to the spirit. Then we will grow Christ and be transformed. If we remain in the spirit, regardless of our environment or circumstances, we will be taken over by the Spirit and become different persons. Then there will be the real possibility for us to have the church life. The only possibility for us to be built up into the temple of God is for us to be in the spirit. We are one in the spirit because in our spirit there is nothing except Christ, and Christ is everything. When we have Christ, we have love and patience. When we have Christ, we have everything.

THE PRACTICALITY OF THE CHURCH LIFE BEING WITH OUR BODY

If we are in the spirit, we will use our physical body in a proper way. We need to let the Spirit take over our whole being; then we will know how to use our body. The possibility for the church life is in our spirit, but the practicality of the church life is with our body. In 1 Corinthians 2 and 3 Paul deals with the spirit, the soul, and the flesh, and in chapter six he deals with our physical body. If we are going to have a proper church life, we have to use our body in the right way.

If you are careless in the way that you dress, you are misusing your body. Your body is for Christ, and Christ is for your body (v. 13). People in the world like to stay up late, making the day the night and the night the day. If we are like this, it will be difficult for us to have a time with the Lord in the morning. In this matter, we misuse our body. We have to be in the spirit to control our body and use it in the proper way.

Chapter six covers the sins of fornication and of eating in excess (v. 13). If we eat at restaurants often, we are misusing our body because that is not healthy for us. We have to be delivered from many old habits by which we misuse our body. Everything concerning the way we eat, dress, and live for our physical existence has to be proper. Our body should be absolutely for the Lord and for nothing else.

We need to learn the lesson of having our spirit strengthened by the Lord, our soul saturated with the Lord, and our body controlled by the Lord. Then there will be the possibility and the practicality for us to have the church life. Then the church can be built up as the temple of God, and we can glorify God in our body in a corporate way (v. 20). We will be the living members of the Body of Christ in our bodies with our spirit strengthened and all the parts of our soul saturated with the Spirit.

CHAPTER SIX

FOUR LINES IN FIRST CORINTHIANS

Scripture Reading: 1 Cor. 1:5, 7; 2:14-15; 3:1, 3; 4:21; 8:1b; 12:31—13:1, 3, 8; 14:1, 37; 16:18, 24

If we are going to experience the things mentioned in 1 Corinthians, we have to see that in this book, four lines are presented to us: the line of Christ, the line of the gifts, the line of the spirit, and the line of the church.

THE LINE OF CHRIST

The first line is the line of Christ. Chapter one says that God has called us into the fellowship, the participation, the enjoyment, of Christ (v. 9). God's intention is that we all may share Christ, partake of Christ, and enjoy Christ as everything to us. Christ is the power of God and the wisdom of God (v. 24). He has been made to us righteousness for our past, sanctification for our present, and redemption for our future (v. 30).

In chapter two Christ is the Lord of glory (v. 8) and the depths of God (v. 10). In chapter three He is the foundation (v. 11). In chapter five He is the Passover (v. 7) and the unleavened bread (v. 8). In chapter ten He is the spiritual food, the spiritual drink, and the spiritual rock (vv. 3-4). In chapter eleven Christ is the Head (v. 3). In chapter twelve He is the Body (v. 12). Finally, in chapter fifteen He is the firstfruits (vv. 20, 23), the second man (v. 47), the last Adam (v. 45), and the life-giving Spirit. He is the first, the second, and the last.

Christ is everything, and this all-inclusive Christ became a life-giving Spirit. This life-giving Spirit indwells our spirit, so he who is joined to the Lord is one spirit (6:17). Today all the items of what Christ is are the elements, the components, of the life-giving Spirit, who dwells in our spirit to be our portion.

THE LINE OF THE GIFTS

The second line in 1 Corinthians is the line of the gifts. This line is not very positive. Rather, in a certain sense, it may be considered as negative. In chapter one Paul said that the Corinthians had been enriched by Christ in everything, especially "in all utterance and all knowledge" (v. 5). He did not say that they were rich in life, in the spirit, or in the experience of Christ. They were rich in speaking and in knowledge in the mind. Furthermore, the Corinthians practiced the miraculous, outward gifts such as healing, speaking in tongues, etc., mentioned in chapters twelve and fourteen. But they were still infants in Christ. They were not only fleshly but even fleshy (3:1).

In chapter twelve Paul said that there are varieties of gifts (v. 4). The gifts are many in number, but at the end of chapter twelve Paul advised the Corinthians to earnestly desire the greater gifts. Of the nine gifts which Paul listed in chapter twelve as the manifestation of the Spirit, speaking in tongues and interpretation of tongues are listed last because they are not the best gifts (vv. 7-10). Then at the end of chapter twelve Paul spoke of the placing of the gifts. He said, "And God has placed some in the church: first apostles, second prophets, third teachers; then works of power, then gifts of healing, helps, administrations, various kinds of tongues" (v. 28). Notice that various kinds of tongues are listed last. Paul went on to say, "Are all apostles? Are all prophets? Are all teachers? Do all have works of power? Do all have gifts of healing? Do all speak in tongues? Do all interpret tongues? But earnestly desire the greater gifts" (vv. 29-31a). Speaking in tongues and interpretation of tongues are again, for the third time, listed last in Paul's writing because they render the least profit to the church (14:4-6, 19).

Then Paul said, "And moreover I show to you a most excellent way" (12:31b). There is something more excellent than the best gifts. The excellent way is love, which is fully defined in chapter thirteen. Speaking in tongues is listed last on Paul's positive lists. Then on his negative list in chapter thirteen, it is listed first. Verse 1 says, "If I speak in the tongues of men and of angels but do not have love, I have become sounding brass or a clanging cymbal." Sounding brass and a clanging cymbal give sounds without life. This is a genuine illustration of tongue-speaking.

Verse 2 says, "And if I have the gift of prophecy and know all mysteries and all knowledge, and if I have all faith so as to remove mountains, but do not have love, I am nothing." Without love we are nothing. Verse 3 says, "And if I dole out all my possessions to feed others, and if I deliver up my body that I may boast, but do not have love, I profit nothing." This shows that if we have the gifts or do anything without love, there is a great lack. We need the gifts plus love. In verse 8 Paul said, "Love never falls away. But whether prophecies, they will be rendered useless; or tongues, they will cease; or knowledge, it will be rendered useless." Love never fails.

People always associate love with the heart. But Paul puts love with the spirit in 1 Corinthians. In 4:21 he spoke of coming to them either with a rod or in love and a spirit of meekness. Love is even deeper than the heart. Love is in the spirit, because it is in our spirit that Christ dwells. The real love, which is the expression of Christ, goes with our spirit because Christ is in our spirit. In 16:18 Paul said that his spirit had been refreshed. Then in verse 24 he said, "My love in Christ Jesus be with you all." His spirit was refreshed and his love was with them. Love goes along with our spirit. If our love is merely out of our heart, that is a natural love, not the divine love which is the expression of Christ. The love which is the expression of Christ comes out of our spirit.

In chapter fourteen Paul charges us, "Pursue love, and desire earnestly spiritual gifts, but especially that you may prophesy" (v. 1). This shows that the apostle Paul was a balanced person. He said to pursue love and desire spiritual gifts, but he made clear that we need to desire the best gift, which is to prophesy. The most important thing, however, is to pursue love. The Corinthians had the gifts but they were short of love in the spirit. Love is the very God embodied in Christ who lives in our spirit.

THE LINE OF THE SPIRIT

The third line in 1 Corinthians is the line of the spirit. Here we are referring to the human spirit and the Holy Spirit. In chapter five Paul told the Corinthians that when they came together, he would meet with them, not in his body but in his spirit. He said, "When you and my spirit have been assembled..." (v. 4). In this assembly he judged a sinful person in the name of the Lord, in the spirit, and in power by delivering such a one to Satan (v. 5).

Paul was a man who behaved in his spirit. In chapter four Paul asked them whether he should come to them with a rod or in love and in a spirit of meekness. When he came to them the first time, he came in demonstration of the Spirit by the exercise of his spirit (2:4). Chapter seven also shows that he was a man in his spirit. In this chapter he was one with the Lord to such a degree that even when he gave his own opinion, he had the Spirit of God.

To be a spiritual man does not mean that you have the Holy Spirit descending on you in a miraculous way to speak in tongues. Balaam's donkey miraculously spoke in tongues, that is, in a human tongue, but his donkey was not spiritual (Num. 22:28-30). Paul, however, was genuinely spiritual. He said in chapter seven that he did not have the Lord's commandment, but as one who had obtained the Lord's mercy, he gave his opinion (v. 25). His opinion became a part of the divine revelation in the Bible. At the end of chapter seven he said, "I think that I also have the Spirit of God" (v. 40). It seems that he was not so sure that he was in the spirit. This shows that to be a spiritual person is to be very human. Many Christians think that to be spiritual one must be angelic, but that is not a spiritual man. A spiritual man is very human in the spirit.

The word spiritual is used a number of times in 1 Corinthians. Paul said in chapter two that the spiritual man discerns all things (v. 15). In chapter three he said that he could not speak to the Corinthians as to spiritual men (v. 1). In chapter nine he said that he sowed spiritual things (v. 11). In chapter ten he spoke of the spiritual food, spiritual drink, and spiritual rock (vv. 3-4). Then in chapter fourteen he spoke of those who think they are spiritual (v. 37).

In order to be spiritual, we always have to exercise our spirit. We always have to walk, behave, and have our being in our spirit. If we are going to be humble, we must be humble in the spirit. Actually, if you live and walk in the spirit, you will be humble without any consciousness of your humility. You will have the reality of being humble without having the consciousness of it. We are also told in the Bible to love one another, but our love may be a soulish love, a natural love. Such love is not the spiritual, divine love which is God Himself embodied in Christ to dwell in our spirit and to be expressed through our spirit. We must love one another in the spirit.

THE LINE OF THE CHURCH

The fourth line in 1 Corinthians is the line of the church. This is a book written to the local church at Corinth (1:2). In this book there is a definite church-consciousness. Whatever Paul said was for the church.

Today the Lord's desire is to recover the proper church life. From the time of Martin Luther, the Lord began His recovery work in a definite way. Within the Lord's recovery there have been four main categories of things: 1) the teachings or doctrines of fundamentalism; 2) the gifts of Pentecostalism; 3) the preaching and spreading of the gospel of evangelicalism; and 4) the inner life. The Lord's recovery has passed through these stages to reach the present-day recovery of the local churches. All the previous recovery work is for this present-day recovery, the building up of the local churches for the building up of the Body of Christ. We need to take Christ as our inner life for the building up of the church.

We also need to see the difference between the gifts and life. Balaam's donkey speaking a human language was a gift, but that did not change the donkey's life. There was no change in life, but there was a change in speaking ability.

Some think that the more gifts they have, the more life they have. But a gift is an enablement or ability for service. It is not life. First Corinthians 13 confirms this. This chapter tells us that everything is empty without love, and love is the expression of Christ as life. If you have the gift of speaking in tongues without love, you are as sounding brass and a clanging cymbal, making empty sounds without life (v. 1).

Gifts are outward. They are the outward endowments of God to enable and equip us for His service. But in addition to these gifts, we need the inward life. The Corinthians had the gifts, but they were short of life. In fact, they were still babes, with hardly any growth in life. They were not only soulish but also fleshly and even fleshy. They misused their gifts because of the shortage of life. They were short of love, which is the expression of life. The gifts are the outward abilities, but life is the inward spiritual essence, which is Christ Himself.

In order to realize life, we have to learn how to exercise our spirit, because the essence of life is Christ Himself. Today Christ is the life-giving Spirit who indwells our spirit, so we have to learn to walk, to behave, and to have our being in our spirit. Never do anything according to what you think, what you like, or what you decide. But always have your being in your spirit. You have to renounce and reject your smart mind, your loving emotions, and your strong will. If you behave yourself in these parts of your soul, you are a soulish man and you are through with Christ. Your behavior will become an insulation between you and Christ. It is not a matter of whether we are good or bad. It is a matter of whether or not we are one with Christ. You may do good things and yet be insulated from Christ. You have to remain in the spirit to be spiritual, not soulish, fleshly, or fleshy.

We can practice the church life and build up the church life only by living in our spirit. Christianity has been divided by teachings, doctrines, and by gifts. Also, the church cannot be built up by good speakers. Many good speakers today minister very little of Christ. We need to enjoy, experience, and partake of Christ and then minister what we have experienced to others. If we enjoy Christ in the spirit and minister Christ to one another, the local church will be built up and there will be no division. We will have the oneness of Philadelphia with the real brotherly love. As long as Christ is enjoyed and ministered, the church will grow up with the nourishment of Christ. Today we are in the age of the recovery of the local churches by Christ being enjoyed by us to be our nourishment for our growth in life.

CHAPTER SEVEN

THE EXPERIENCE OF CHRIST IN SECOND CORINTHIANS

Scripture Reading: 2 Cor. 1:19; 2:14-15; 3:3, 18; 4:4-7, 10-11; 5:14-17, 21; 8:9; 10:1, 5; 11:2-3, 10; 12:9; 13:3-5, 14

In the previous chapter, we saw the four lines in 1 Corinthians. Now we want to compare what has been spoken concerning Christ in 1 Corinthians with what Paul said in 2 Corinthians.

Second Corinthians gives us a real picture of Christ in our experience in an improved way. In the first Epistle, the aspects concerning Christ are mentioned more or less in a doctrinal way. But we need all these aspects in order to go on to the deeper experience of Christ seen in Paul's second Epistle. First, we have the doctrinal aspects of Christ. Then we have the Christ in our experience.

CHRIST AS THE YES

In 2 Corinthians 1:19 Paul said, "For the Son of God, Jesus Christ, who was preached among you through us, through me and Silvanus and Timothy, did not become yes and no, but our word has become yes in Him." We can realize that Paul has turned from the doctrinal side to the experiential side. Christ is not yes and no. Christ is yes in your experience, not in your understanding. We can say that Christ is the Yes only by our experience.

A CAPTIVE OF CHRIST

In 2:14 Paul said, "But thanks be to God, who always leads us in triumph in the Christ and manifests the savor of the knowledge of Him through us in every place." If you are going to enjoy and experience Christ, you have to be a captive. You

have to be captured. You may say that Christ is the power
and wisdom of God (1 Cor. 1:24), but if you are going to experience Christ as God's power and wisdom, you have to be a
captive. Do you like to be captured? You have to be led by
Christ in His train of vanquished foes (Eph. 4:8). In this universe God is celebrating Christ's victory with a triumphal
procession of vanquished foes. You must be one of these
defeated and captured foes.

Saul of Tarsus was a strong, ambitious young man who
was against Christ. When the Lord met him on the road to
Damascus, He said to Saul, "It is hard for you to kick against
the goads" (Acts 26:14). A goad on a plow is a sharp-pointed
stick used to subdue and prod an ox yoked to the plow. While
Saul was kicking against the goads, the Lord was laughing at
him in the heavens (Psa. 2:4). Actually, Saul was under the
Lord's control. This rebel was made an apostle by being captured by Christ. God led him from city to city as a captive to
celebrate the victory of Christ. Paul could tell people, "I once
was a rebel, but now I am a captive!" This is a celebration.
Saul was a rebel against Christ, but he became captured by
Christ. He went from city to city to preach Christ as one in
the train of vanquished foes to celebrate the victory of Christ.

We have to apply this experience to ourselves. Before we
preach Christ to others, we have to be captured by Christ.
While we are preaching, others should have the impression
that we are captives in the celebrating train of vanquished
foes. We can tell people how we used to be rebellious against
Christ, but now we are the captives of Christ. This will
become a sweet savor, a sweet odor of Christ, which can be
smelled by others (2 Cor. 2:15-16). The real preaching is not a
matter of mere speaking. It is a matter of showing forth that
we are being led as captives in Christ's train of vanquished
foes. When we are such captives, we can experience Christ in
a deeper way. This is the pure experience of Christ to make us
a fragrance of Christ to God (v. 15).

A LETTER OF CHRIST

In 2 Corinthians 3:3 Paul said, "Since you are being manifested that you are a letter of Christ ministered by us,

inscribed not with ink but with the Spirit of the living God; not in tablets of stone but in tablets of hearts of flesh." Christ has to be written into us, to be wrought into us, to make us the living letters of Christ. People should be able to read Christ on our being. We may preach about Christ, but how much of Christ can people read on us? When people observe the way that we live, can they read Christ?

This shows again that 2 Corinthians is not a book of doctrine but a book of experience. We need to be captives of Christ and letters of Christ. We need more of Christ written upon us. This means we need more of Christ wrought into us. Christ has to be wrought into our thinking, our loving, our choosing, and into our entire being. This is not a matter of doctrine. It is absolutely a matter of experience.

A MIRROR OF CHRIST

Paul told us that we are captives of Christ and letters of Christ. Then in 3:18 he told us that we are a mirror of Christ. As a mirror of Christ, we need to behold Him that we may reflect Him. By beholding and reflecting Him, we are being transformed into His image from one degree of glory to another. This is a matter of experience. In order to behold Christ, we need an unveiled face. When all the veils are taken away, the mirror can behold the image with an unveiled face. Then the mirror can reflect the image. We need all the veils to be taken away from us so that we can have an open spirit to look at Christ. Then we will be transformed from glory to glory into His image.

THE TREASURE IN EARTHEN VESSELS

In 4:7 Paul said that we have this treasure in earthen vessels. Christ is the treasure, and we are the earthen vessels to contain Him. Chapter four goes on to reveal that we need to be broken, consumed, and reduced so that Christ as the treasure can be manifested from within us (vv. 8-12, 16-17). Do not think that if you learn more doctrines or receive more gifts, you will grow. We need to see that to grow in life is to be reduced.

Chapter four speaks of the "putting to death of Jesus," or

the killing of Jesus (v. 10). Christ is killing us. He is not only the life-giving Spirit but also the killing Spirit. Christ is always putting us to death to reduce and consume us in our outer man, our natural man, so that our inner man may have the opportunity to develop and be renewed (v. 16). You may think that if you have learned all the doctrines in the Bible, you have grown up. But you are not grown-up; you are puffed up (1 Cor. 8:1). The real growth is to be reduced. We need to be reduced, to be broken. The outer man is being consumed so that the inner man may be renewed day by day. This is the real growth in life. The killing of Jesus accomplishes the reducing of our natural life.

If everything in our environment were right with us, we could not be reduced. We need the wrong things to reduce us. God sovereignly arranges our environment to allow many wrong things to happen to us. This is not Christ in doctrine, but Christ in our killing experience and even painful experience. Paul said that he experienced the killing of Jesus that the life of Jesus could be manifested in his body (2 Cor. 4:10). Without this killing, we cannot enjoy Christ's life.

THE LOVE OF CHRIST
CONSTRAINING US TO LIVE TO CHRIST

In 2 Corinthians 5 Paul spoke of the love of Christ constraining us to live to Christ. Verses 14 and 15 say, "For the love of Christ constrains us because we have judged this, that One died for all, therefore all died; and He died for all that those who live may no longer live to themselves but to Him who died for them and has been raised." We have to be constrained to such an extent that we lose ourselves, forget about ourselves, and live to Christ.

GOD'S RIGHTEOUSNESS IN CHRIST

Verse 21 says that Christ was made sin and that we are made the righteousness of God in Him. This does not mean that we are righteous, but that we are righteousness itself through the redemption of Christ. We were sin itself. To turn sin into righteousness required much work. Christ was made sin for us to be judged and done away with by God that we might become God's righteousness in Christ.

THE MEEKNESS AND GENTLENESS OF CHRIST

Chapter ten speaks of Paul's experience of the meekness and gentleness of Christ (v. 1). This cannot be worked out by teaching. Someone may tell you to look at how gentle and meek Christ was on earth and that you need to learn of Him, but this does not work. We need Christ wrought into us so that His meekness and gentleness can be ours.

TAKING CAPTIVE EVERY THOUGHT
UNTO THE OBEDIENCE OF CHRIST

In 10:5 Paul said, "As we overthrow reasonings and every high thing rising up against the knowledge of God, and take captive every thought unto the obedience of Christ." Our thoughts have to be brought into captivity. They must be taken captive to obey Christ. Often, we are rebellious in our mind. Our mind is wild, natural, rebellious, and unrenewed. This is why we need to be transformed by the renewing of the mind (Rom. 12:2). By being renewed, our mind will be subdued and brought into captivity unto the obedience of Christ. How much has our mind been renewed, subdued, and captured? This is not a matter of doctrine but of experience.

THE VIRGINS OF CHRIST

Thus far, we have seen that we are the captives of Christ, the letters of Christ, the mirrors of Christ, and the vessels of Christ. Chapter eleven goes on to tell us that we are the virgins of Christ who have been betrothed to Christ (v. 2). To marry someone is not a matter of doctrine but a matter of experience. Do we have the real experience of being a virgin to Christ?

THE TRUTHFULNESS OF CHRIST

In 11:10 Paul said that the truthfulness of Christ was in him. Because Paul lived by Christ, whatever Christ is became his virtue in his behavior. This virtue of truthfulness has to be wrought into us.

THE GRACE OF CHRIST

In 12:9 the Lord told Paul, "My grace is sufficient for you." At that time Paul had a thorn which was piercing him, troubling him, hurting him, and giving him pain all the time (v. 7). He asked the Lord three times to remove this thorn (v. 8), but the Lord left the thorn with him so that he might experience the Lord's sufficient grace. If the Lord had taken away the thorn, Paul could not have experienced His sufficient grace.

CHRIST SPEAKING IN ME

In chapter thirteen Paul said that Christ was speaking in him (v. 3). This is not a doctrine. Have you experienced Christ speaking within you?

BEING WEAK IN CHRIST THAT
HE MIGHT BE POWERFUL WITHIN US

This speaking Christ within us is powerful, not weak. But if we are to experience Christ as power, we have to learn how to be weak in Him (v. 4). We are always taught to be strong, but we have to learn how to be weak. We are too strong in ourselves, in our natural man. We need to learn to be weak that Christ might be powerful within us.

THE GRACE OF CHRIST,
THE LOVE OF GOD, AND THE FELLOWSHIP
OF THE HOLY SPIRIT BEING WITH US ALL

Paul concluded 2 Corinthians by saying, "The grace of the Lord Jesus Christ and the love of God and the fellowship of the Holy Spirit be with you all." The grace of Christ is the full enjoyment of Christ. Paul wanted this enjoyment along with the love of God and the fellowship of the Spirit to be with us in our experience.

THE DEEPER EXPERIENCE OF CHRIST

Now that we have seen the verses related to Christ in 2 Corinthians, we can realize that every aspect in this Epistle is absolutely a matter of experience. In 1 Corinthians we saw that there are four lines: the line of Christ, the line of the gifts, the line of the spirit, and the line of the church. In 2 Corinthians the line of Christ is greatly enriched and developed in experience. We can also see the line of the spirit and the line of the church in 2 Corinthians. But the line of the gifts is not here. Healings, miracles, speaking in tongues, interpretation of tongues, and knowledge are not mentioned in 2 Corinthians.

The Lord did use Paul to perform some miracles, but the Lord would not perform a miracle to remove the thorn in his flesh. The Lord kept the thorn with Paul so that he might learn to experience the Lord's sufficient grace. A husband might ask the Lord to change his wife, but the Lord would keep his wife the same so that he might learn to experience Christ as grace. If the Lord changed this brother's wife, there would be no opportunity for him to experience the Lord as the sufficient grace. Do you want to have a better wife or the sufficient grace? The Lord allows our spouse, our children, and our entire environment to trouble us so that we will have the chance to experience Christ as the sufficient grace.

There are no miraculous things in 2 Corinthians because this is a book on the deeper experience of Christ. When we are in the elementary stage, we may desire the gifts, but when we are advanced in Christ, we care for the deeper experiences of Christ. Second Corinthians does not speak of miracles and gifts increasing with us. Instead, it speaks of Christ increasing within us all the time through many sufferings.

Everything in 2 Corinthians has been developed in a deeper way, and all of the outward teachings and gifts are over. I am not saying that the gifts are unnecessary or that the teachings are useless. They are good for the beginning. But once something has been started through the teachings and gifts, you have to be turned from them. Doctrinal teachings and gifts will divide.

If our gifts are steadily increasing, after a short time we will be divided by these increasing gifts. Gifts are good for the start. But once you have the start through the gifts, you have to be turned to the indwelling Christ. In 2 Corinthians there are no more gifts. There is just the indwelling Christ to be wrought into us through hardships, trials, troubles, and sufferings. If we mean business with the Lord and go along with the Lord, we will experience Him through sufferings, hardships, and trials.

We can never be divided by the experience of Christ in the spirit, but it is easy to be divided by teachings and gifts. If we pay our attention to increasing the gifts, there is the danger that these increased gifts will become dividers to divide us. Then the local church can never be built up. This is why in 2 Corinthians the gifts are not increasing but they are terminated. Instead, Christ is developing and increasing all the time. This is the way that we can have the real growth in life for the local church to be built up.

The increase of teachings and gifts is not the growth in life. The growth in life is absolutely something of Christ being developed within you and experienced by you. The Body of Christ is built up with the increase and development of Christ, not with the increase of doctrine or with the development of the gifts. May the Lord have mercy upon us that we would be willing to turn away from the elementary gifts. The gifts are elementary things good for the beginning. Once something has been started, we need to turn away from the start to the real experience of Christ Himself.

CHAPTER EIGHT

EXPERIENCING THE SPIRIT
IN SECOND CORINTHIANS

(1)

Scripture Reading: 2 Cor. 1:21-22; 3:3, 6, 8, 17-18; 5:5; 13:14

We have seen that there are four lines in 1 Corinthians: the line of Christ, the line of the gifts, the line of the spirit (including the Holy Spirit), and the line of the church. All except one of these lines, the line of the gifts, is continued in 2 Corinthians. This line is replaced with the line of the ministry, which is formed and produced by the experience of Christ through much suffering. In 2 Corinthians 3 there is the ministry of the Spirit (v. 8), not the gifts of the Spirit. The ministry is not produced overnight. It is produced over time through suffering. If you know the Lord's gracious dealing, you will kiss all the sufferings. Sufferings work out something which is much better than the gifts, that is, the ministry.

We have seen that 1 Corinthians reveals many aspects of Christ more or less in a doctrinal way. Chapter one says the Jews require signs and the Greeks seek wisdom, but Paul preached Christ crucified, and Christ is the power and wisdom of God (vv. 22-24). In chapter two Paul said he made the decision not to know anything except Christ and Christ crucified (v. 2). Then in the following chapters, he went on to reveal more aspects of Christ in a doctrinal way. But when Paul spoke of Christ in 2 Corinthians, he spoke in the way of experience.

THE LINE OF THE SPIRIT IN SECOND CORINTHIANS

First Corinthians, in a sense, is for doctrine. Second

Corinthians is for experience. We can see this when we consider the line of the spirit in these two books. In 1 Corinthians 2 Paul told us that the Spirit reveals the deep things of God to us (v. 10). Then chapter three says that the Spirit dwells within us (v. 16). Chapter twelve speaks of the gifts of the Spirit (vv. 4-11) and says that we have been baptized in the Spirit and are drinking of the one Spirit (v. 13). Chapter fifteen reveals that Christ, as the last Adam, became a life-giving Spirit (v. 45b).

When we consider all these aspects of the Spirit in 1 Corinthians, we can realize that they are mentioned with a lack of experience. Paul's mentioning of the Spirit in 2 Corinthians is more experiential. In chapter one he says that the Spirit is the anointing Spirit and the sealing Spirit. This Spirit is also in our hearts as a pledge, a foretaste (vv. 21-22).

In chapter three there are five aspects of this subjective Spirit. First, He is the writing Spirit (v. 3); then He is the life-giving Spirit (v. 6). He is also the ministering Spirit, who always ministers something of Christ into us (v. 8). He is the liberating Spirit (v. 17) to liberate us from all the things that bind us. He liberates us from the bondage of doctrines, the letter, the written codes and regulations. He delivers us by taking away all the veils so that we can behold and reflect Christ with an unveiled face. Then He is the transforming Spirit. We are being transformed into the glorious image of the Lord from glory to glory, even as from the Lord Spirit (v. 18).

The last verse of 2 Corinthians speaks of the fellowship of the Holy Spirit (13:14). The fellowship here is the transmission. The love of the Father is the source, the grace of the Son is the course, and the fellowship of the Spirit is the transmission that transmits all that Christ is as grace to us with God the Father as love.

Second Corinthians is a book of transmission, not a book of doctrine. The nine aspects of the Spirit we have mentioned above are altogether in the realm of experience. These nine aspects once again are: the anointing Spirit, the sealing Spirit, the pledging Spirit, the writing Spirit, the life-giving Spirit, the ministering Spirit, the liberating Spirit, the transforming Spirit, and the transmitting Spirit. This wonderful Spirit transmits all the riches of Christ with the fullness of the Father into us.

THE ANOINTING SPIRIT

Second Corinthians 1:21 says, "But the One who firmly attaches us with you unto Christ and has anointed us is God." Christ in Greek means "the anointed One." Since we have been attached by God to Christ, the anointed One, we are spontaneously anointed with Him by God. In the previous verses, Paul said that the very Christ whom he ministered to the saints is not yes and no. The Christ he ministered is always yes. He is the Amen in the whole universe (vv. 19-20). Then Paul said that God attaches us firmly unto such a Christ, who is the great Yes and the universal Amen.

God has anointed Him with the oil of exultant joy above His partners (Psa. 45:7; Heb. 1:9). The ointment with which Christ and we are anointed is God Himself. God has painted us, anointed us, with Himself as the divine paint, the divine ointment. The more we are anointed by God, the more of the element of God's divine nature we receive. The anointing is for the imparting of the divine element into us. God imparts all of His divine ingredients and constituents into us by His anointing.

How could we people of flesh be attached to Christ, who is full of the divine nature? The only way is by being anointed. In one sense, all of us who have been regenerated have been attached to Christ. But in our experience, how much we have been attached to Christ depends on the amount of anointing we have received. The more anointing we have, the more we are attached to Christ. Even in our daily walk we can testify of this. If we are living and doing things under the anointing, this anointing teaches us in everything (1 John 2:27). When you walk according to this anointing, you have the sense that at that time you are attached to Christ.

Let us use the example of shopping. If you do not take care of the inner anointing when you go to the department store, and you shop merely according to your likes and dislikes, at that time you are far away from Christ. You are separated from Christ. Instead you should say, "O Lord, deliver me from the satanic system in this department store. If You say no, I say no. If You say yes, I say yes." When you walk in this spirit of prayer, you are behaving and acting according to the inner anointing. At that time you are attached to the anointed One.

Today God is doing a work to attach us to Christ, the anointed One, by anointing us continually with Himself. When we enjoy this anointing, we have the deep sense that we are attached to Christ. We can realize that this is much deeper and finer than the gifts. This is the precious experience which we need daily. The experience of Christ for our transformation is not a matter of the miraculous, supernatural gifts but a matter of the deep, hidden, powerful, and fine anointing. The anointing Spirit day by day anoints us with the ingredients and the constituents of God, the divine elements of God Himself. Day by day if we will simply walk and behave according to this anointing, God will be added into us, imparted into us, more and more.

THE SEALING SPIRIT

We need to go on from being anointed to being sealed. The Spirit is also the sealing Spirit. The sealing forms the divine elements into an impression to express God's image. I am encouraged when I see that God is being formed within many of you (Gal. 4:19). When people contact you, they will have the sense that with you there is the image of God and something of God formed within you.

I can illustrate this by the following story. Once in Shanghai a certain sister came to visit us, and none of us had ever seen her. When we went to the pier to meet her, we were wondering how we would recognize her. As we were watching the persons in the boat, we realized who the sister was. There was a certain kind of image or impression with her, testifying that she must be a child of God.

God has not only anointed us but also sealed us. He has not only imparted His elements into us but has also impressed us with His own image with the form of the living Spirit. This is the deeper experience of the indwelling Spirit. It is not the outward manifestation of the Spirit but the inward impression and sealing of the Spirit.

THE PLEDGING SPIRIT

In 2 Corinthians 1:22 Paul said that God has "given the Spirit in our hearts as a pledge." The pledge is the foretaste. The Spirit is a foretaste, a guarantee, a sample, of the full taste. He is sweet to our spiritual taste. God gives His Spirit to us as a foretaste of what we will inherit of God, affording us a taste beforehand of the full inheritance. When the sisters cook something in the kitchen, they take a foretaste of it. But when they bring it to the table, they take the full taste. Today we are in the kitchen, not at the table. We taste the Spirit as a foretaste, and this is a sample of the full taste of the Spirit to come on a greater scale. We need to enjoy the indwelling Spirit as the foretaste day by day.

This is what we need for the growth in life, for the building up of the Body, and for the real practice of the church life. The more we experience the Spirit in such a hidden, deep, high, rich, and inner way, the more we will be delivered from being divisive. But the more we experience the gifts in an outward way and the more doctrinal teachings we receive, the more puffed up and divisive we will be. This is why division and strife are so prevalent in 1 Corinthians. The Corinthians had knowledge and the gifts, but they were fleshly and divisive, full of strife and envy. A brother who walks under the anointing, who is sealed by the Lord, and who enjoys the foretaste of the Spirit day by day has no possibility of being divisive. The way to build up the Body is not in 1 Corinthians but in 2 Corinthians. The building up of the Body is by the anointing, sealing, and pledging of the Spirit within us.

THE WRITING SPIRIT

Second Corinthians 3:3 says, "Since you are being manifested that you are a letter of Christ ministered by us, inscribed not with ink but with the Spirit of the living God; not in tablets of stone but in tablets of hearts of flesh." The Spirit is the writing Spirit, and we are the letters of Christ. The Spirit is the ink for writing Christ into us. As the divine ink, the Spirit is the Spirit of the living God. There should be something living within us all the time as evidence that

Christ is being written into every part of our inner being. If we are under the Spirit's writing, we have the deep sensation of being living within. Christ is being written into us with the spiritual ink, the Spirit of the living God. This makes us a letter of Christ. All of us should be such a living letter of Christ, that others may read and know Christ in our being. We are under the writing of the Spirit of the living God, and He is engraving Christ into us.

THE LIFE-GIVING SPIRIT

In 2 Corinthians 3:6 Paul said that the letter kills but the Spirit gives life. This means that the Spirit inwardly imparts life into us day by day. We need to always return to our spirit because it is in our spirit that we sense and experience the imparting of life. This revives us and makes us living. If we pay attention to the letter of the Bible, we will be killed. We do not need the regulating of the letter, because we have the regulating of the Spirit within us.

Paul, of course, wrote the church in Corinth with the background of Judaism. Those in Judaism became stuck to the written code of the Old Testament according to the letter. But Paul came and told them something different from this written code. Their eyes were veiled with this written code, so they opposed Paul. They could not see Jesus, the Spirit, or any of the spiritual things, because they were veiled. So the apostle Paul told them that the letter kills. It is the Spirit who gives life, and the Lord is the Spirit (v. 17). They needed to take away all the veils, which means that they had to get rid of their old knowledge of the written code.

In principle it is the same today. Today's Christianity is like Judaism in the sense that the ones there stick themselves to the written code of the Bible, which kills, and not to the living Spirit, who gives life. It is pitiful to keep ourselves under the dead letter, the written code of outward regulations. All the veils of our old knowledge of old doctrines according to the dead letter need to be taken away. We need an unveiled, open face to look at the Lord directly. We care just for the Spirit, not for any doctrinal teaching.

CHAPTER NINE

EXPERIENCING THE SPIRIT
IN SECOND CORINTHIANS

(2)

Scripture Reading: 2 Cor. 3:6, 8, 17-18; 13:14; 1 Cor. 15:45b;
John 6:63; 5:21

We have pointed out that in 1 Corinthians there is mostly
the doctrine concerning Christ, but in the second Epistle there
is the experience and enjoyment of Christ. In the previous
chapter, we began to speak about the aspects of the Spirit
in 2 Corinthians. Whatever is spoken there concerning the
Spirit is not in the way of doctrine but in the way of experience. It tells us something richer and finer than 1 Corinthians
does.

In 1 Corinthians the Spirit is the revealing Spirit, the
gift-dispensing Spirit, and the indwelling Spirit. But 2 Corinthians tells us first that the Spirit is the anointing Spirit
(1:21). The anointing is richer and finer than the revealing.
Suppose a mother just showed her daughter food and did not
serve her the food. I prefer not the showing, the revealing, but
the feeding. Whatever the Lord reveals, He anoints into us.
The revealing is for seeing, and the anointing is for enjoying.

Today's Christians are so much for knowing, for seeing.
They like to listen to messages from good speakers. Paul said
that when the decline of the church worsens, people "will not
tolerate the healthy teaching; but according to their own lusts
they will heap up to themselves teachers, having itching ears"
(2 Tim. 4:3). Paul told the Corinthians that they might have
ten thousand guides, or teachers, but not many fathers (1 Cor.
4:15). Teachers pass on knowledge; fathers impart life. What

we need today is not teachers but fathers. Those with itching ears like to heap up teachers to themselves. They like only to know, to see.

But after the seeing in 1 Corinthians, we must come to the anointing in 2 Corinthians. The Spirit in 2 Corinthians is not the teaching Spirit but the anointing Spirit. The Holy Spirit anoints us with the divine essence, just like a painter paints a house with the essence of paint. The Spirit anoints us with the essence of God's nature, with the substance of what God is. The more He anoints us, the more of God we have.

We have also seen that the Spirit is the sealing Spirit (1:22). The anointing brings in the essence, and the sealing shapes what the anointing brings in into a definite form and image. When you mark a piece of paper with a seal, there is a definite form, an image, on that paper. The anointing Spirit brings in the riches of God's fullness. Then the sealing Spirit shapes them into a form which gives people an impression. When you are sealed by the Spirit, you have the image of God, the impression of God, and the likeness of God. The anointing Spirit brings in all the riches of the Godhead so that we have something substantial. Then the sealing Spirit follows to make this substance into a form so that we have the image, impression, and likeness of God.

Following this the Spirit becomes the pledge, the foretaste, the earnest, the down payment, the first installment, the sample, for us to taste (v. 22). In the kitchen the sisters who cook have the foretaste of the things they cook. But when the food is put on the table, they have the full taste. Today the Holy Spirit who anoints us and seals us is for us to taste. This is more subjective. Still, what we are enjoying today is the small taste in the kitchen, not the full taste at the dining table. The dining table will come some day, and we all will be there tasting the Spirit in His fullness. But praise Him, today we have the foretaste! We need to taste the Spirit continually.

He is also the writing Spirit. We are the living letters of Christ composed with Christ as the content, and the Spirit is the writing ink (3:3). The Spirit is writing Christ into us. This is not an outward teaching or an objective revealing but an inward, subjective writing of Christ into our being.

Second Corinthians also says that the Spirit gives life. He is the Life-giver (3:6). God has made us the sufficient ministers of the new covenant, not of the letter but of the Spirit. People think that if they are going to be a minister, they have to go to seminary to be taught. But Paul said that he was a minister "not of the letter but of the Spirit." What a difference in concept! The letter here refers to the written code or regulations. We can be outwardly regulated with no life.

The Pharisees, the scribes, and the Jewish leaders at Jesus' time knew all the right doctrines in the Old Testament. Herod called for the chief priests and scribes and asked them where the Christ was to be born. Right away they gave him the right doctrine by telling him that the place would be Bethlehem (Matt. 2:4-6). They had this doctrinal knowledge, but they would not go to Christ. The magi, however, went to contact Christ, not just according to the right teaching but according to the living star (v. 9). The Lord Jesus told the Jewish religionists that they researched the Bible, but they would not come to Him for life (John 5:39-40). The written code kills and deadens, but the Spirit gives life.

Life is the Triune God flowing Himself out. It is the living flow of the Triune God. The picture of this is in Revelation 22, where we see the throne of God and of the Lamb, and out of the throne flows the river of water of life (v. 1). In this river grows the tree of life (v. 2). Life is divine, eternal, flowing, and living. People may be bothered at the noise in our meetings, but the Bible tells us to make a joyful noise to the Lord (Psa. 100:1). The quietest place is the cemetery, the place full of dead people. The Christian life and the church life are not a matter of what is right or wrong, but a matter of what is dead or living. The written code kills, but the living and flowing Spirit gives life. Today it is not a matter of the tree of the knowledge of good and evil, right and wrong. Today is the day of life, the day of the tree of life.

In John 5:21 the Lord said, "For just as the Father raises the dead and gives them life, so also the Son gives life to whom He wills." Thus, we see that the Father gives life, the Son gives life, and the Spirit gives life. Even the word spoken by the Lord gives life. He said that the words that He spoke were spirit and life (John 6:63). The word here is the living, instant, and present word, not the constant Word. The living, present word of the Lord is spirit and life.

Many times when you try to study the Bible, you are deadened because you get a lot of doctrinal knowledge without life. We need to study and read the Bible prayerfully with the exercise of our spirit. The mental reading kills, but the prayerful reading gives life. The more you read the Bible prayerfully, the more you have the deep sense that something within you is flowing, quickening, reviving, enlightening, and strengthening. The Concordant Literal New Testament translation of 2 Corinthians 3:6 says that the Spirit is "vivifying." The more you read the Word prayerfully, the more you are vivified. When you read the Word mentally, you are mortified, but when you read the Word prayerfully, you are vivified. Whether you will be vivified or mortified depends upon the way you take to read the Bible.

Even the Bible can be a dead, written code to us if we do not come to Christ Himself to receive life. We need more life, not more knowledge. We need to be more and more vivified. We can be vivified by pray-reading the Lord's Word. Life is what we need. The Spirit is not the Spirit of doctrine but the Spirit of reality, who is Christ Himself as life. The more we contact the Spirit, the more we are vivified.

The life-giving Spirit, the vivifying Spirit, is Christ Himself. Verse 6 of 2 Corinthians 3 says that the Spirit gives life. Darby puts verses 7 through 16 in parentheses, indicating that verse 17 directly continues verse 6. Verse 17 says that the Lord is the Spirit. Thus, the Spirit who gives life is Christ the Lord. Christ as the last Adam became the life-giving Spirit (1 Cor. 15:45b).

I would like to point out what Dean Alford said concerning 2 Corinthians 3:16-17:

> The Lord of v. 16, is the Spirit...which giveth life, v. 6: meaning, "the Lord," as here spoken of, "Christ," "is the Spirit," is identical with the Holy Spirit... Christ, here, is the Spirit of Christ.

Let us also read what M. R. Vincent had to say about this passage of Scripture:

> The Lord Christ of v. 16 is the Spirit who pervades and animates the new covenant of which we are ministers (v. 6)....

We may wonder how Christ, as Dean Alford pointed out, could be the Spirit of Christ. We may not be able to understand this, but we simply need to say amen to what the Bible says. Hebrews 1:8 refers to Christ the Son as God, and then verse 9 says that God is His God. This is the mystery of the Divine Trinity. We cannot fully comprehend such a mystery, but we can accept it. The Bible says that Christ as the last Adam became a life-giving Spirit, that the Lord is the Spirit who gives life, and that he who is joined to the Lord is one spirit (1 Cor. 6:17). This is not my teaching, but my quotation of the Bible. This is not my invention, but my discovery.

Now that we have seen the anointing Spirit, the sealing Spirit, the pledging Spirit, the writing Spirit, and the life-giving Spirit, let us go on to see the remaining aspects of the Spirit in 2 Corinthians.

THE MINISTERING SPIRIT

The life-giving Spirit is also the ministering Spirit. Second Corinthians 3:8 speaks of the ministry of the Spirit. In this second Epistle, the gifts of the Spirit are replaced with the ministry of the Spirit. Balaam's donkey received the gift of speaking in a human language, of speaking in tongues, but that was not a ministry. The donkey received such a gift suddenly, but a ministry takes time to be built up. A ministry is produced in a person because Christ has been wrought into him for many years, not just overnight. The ministry is produced through years of the Lord's working, dealing, and building up bit by bit.

Sometimes when a saint speaks, you can realize he is exercising his gift. But when another saint speaks, you realize that he has a real ministry because something has been built and wrought into his being through many sufferings over a period of time. Once something of Christ has been wrought

into you, nothing can take it away. When you experience
Christ through sufferings, the ministry of Christ with you is
enriched, strengthened, and uplifted. Then what you speak
comes out of your constitution, your very being. This is not a
gift but a ministry.

When the apostle Paul ministered, he was not merely
exercising his gift. Paul ministered Christ so richly because
something of Christ had been wrought into him and built into
him to become one with him. Actually, Paul was the ministry.
Not only his word but also his person was the ministry. The
ministry does not minister knowledge, doctrine, or the expo-
sition of the Bible. It ministers the riches of Christ. The
ministry of the Spirit imparts all that Christ is into us. If you
listen to certain speakers, you may feel that you only receive
knowledge without anything watering or feeding you. But you
may listen to someone who is not so eloquent, yet you have
the deep feeling that you are nourished, watered, and vivified.
This is the ministry of the Spirit. This is the Spirit of life
ministering Christ into you.

The Spirit is the reality of what Christ is. Christ is life.
If you do not have the Spirit, you do not have the reality of
life. Christ is light. If you do not have the Spirit, you do not
have the reality of light. Christ is love. If you do not have the
Spirit, you do not have the reality of love. Christ is every-
thing. If you do not have the Spirit, you do not have anything.
Instead, you have mere biblical terminology without reality.
The reality of every item of Christ's riches is the Spirit. The
Lord said that all that the Father is and has was given to
Him, and whatever He received was passed on to the Spirit of
reality. Then the Spirit of reality passes on what He has to us
(John 16:13-15). This means that He leads us into all the real-
ity of what Christ is. He ministers Christ as everything into
us.

THE LIBERATING SPIRIT

Second Corinthians 3:17 says, "And the Lord is the Spirit;
and where the Spirit of the Lord is, there is freedom." The
freedom mentioned here is the freedom, the liberty, from
the letter of the law under the veil (Gal. 2:4; 5:1). The Spirit

liberates us from the written code, the written regulations. The Judaizers knew the teachings and doctrines of the Old Testament, but these became layers of veils to them. They knew a lot, but they did not see anything.

We need an unveiled face to see the glorious Christ. What we need today is not more knowing but more seeing. We need to be liberated from the bondage of the deadening, blinding written code. Some of us have been overloaded with biblical knowledge. We need to be unloaded and emptied so that we can freshly receive Christ Himself in the newness of His living presence. When we have an unveiled face, we are liberated from religion, old doctrines, and traditions to behold and reflect the living Christ.

THE TRANSFORMING SPIRIT

As we behold Christ face to face, we mirror Him, and we are being transformed into His image from one degree of glory to another degree. This is altogether from the Lord Spirit (2 Cor. 3:18). Thus, we have the liberation and the transformation.

First Corinthians tells us that Christ became a life-giving Spirit, but it does not tell us how He gives life. The details are in 2 Corinthians. The life-giving is the anointing, the sealing, the pledging, the writing, the ministering of Christ, the liberating from the bondage of religion and legal doctrines, and the transforming into the Lord's image. Transformation is not an outward change but an inward, metabolic change by the discharge of our old element and the infusion of the Lord's new element.

THE TRANSMITTING SPIRIT

Second Corinthians concludes with Paul saying, "The grace of the Lord Jesus Christ and the love of God and the fellowship of the Holy Spirit be with you all" (13:14). This is not a benediction but a transmission. Love is the source, the fountain; grace is the course, the spring; and the fellowship is the river, the flow, to transmit all that Christ is with all the fullness of God into us. God is love, and this love is being transmitted as grace to us by the Spirit who is the

Transmitter. All that God is as love is in Christ. Love is embodied in grace. Love is something in the heart, but grace is the expression of love. Grace comes out of love, and this grace is being transmitted into us by the Spirit. Love, grace, and fellowship are not three separate entities, but one thing in three stages. God is in Christ, and Christ is the Spirit. Christ is God's embodiment, and the Spirit is Christ's reality. The Spirit is the transmission of Christ, who is the embodiment of God. Second Corinthians concludes with the transmitting, communicating, and flowing Spirit.

May the Lord have mercy upon us. We need the experience of the Spirit which Paul spoke of in 2 Corinthians. We need the anointing Spirit, the sealing Spirit, the pledging Spirit, the writing Spirit, the life-giving Spirit, the ministering Spirit, the liberating Spirit, the transforming Spirit, and the transmitting, flowing Spirit.

CHAPTER TEN

THE ANOINTING OF THE COMPOUND SPIRIT

Scripture Reading: Exo. 30:23-26, 29, 30; 2 Cor. 1:21; 1 John 2:20, 27

We have pointed out that the aspects of the Spirit mentioned in 2 Corinthians are different from those mentioned in 1 Corinthians. This means that there are different kinds of experiences of the same Spirit. In 1 Corinthians the Spirit is the revealing, gift-dispensing, and indwelling Spirit. But 2 Corinthians shows us some deeper experiences of the same Spirit. We have seen that in this second Epistle there are nine aspects of the substantial and subjective work of the Holy Spirit within us: the anointing, sealing, guaranteeing, writing, life-giving, ministering, liberating, transforming, and transmitting. Ultimately, the Spirit transmits all that Christ is with the fullness of the Godhead into us. These aspects are very deep, substantial, and subjective. In this chapter we would like to say more concerning the anointing aspect of the Spirit.

THE ANOINTING

In the New Testament we are told that we have a wonderful thing called the anointing (1 John 2:20, 27). God has anointed us and has attached us unto the anointed One (2 Cor. 1:21). The anointed One is Christ, the Son of God, whom God has anointed above all His partners, His companions (Heb. 1:9). By being attached to Him we all have been anointed. Now we share the anointing from the Holy One. This anointing abides in us and teaches us in everything. The anointing is the moving of the ointment, the moving of the Spirit within us.

THE COMPOUND OINTMENT

We need to consider the difference between oil and oint-ment, because both of them typify the Spirit. Exodus 30 speaks of both olive oil and the compound ointment (vv. 24-25). The oil is composed of only one element, the element of the olive, but the ointment is composed of oil plus a number of elements. The compound ointment is composed of one basic element, olive oil, blended and compounded together with four kinds of spices. This compound ointment in Exodus 30 is a wonderful picture and type of the all-inclusive, compound Spirit in the New Testament (Phil. 1:19).

THE INGREDIENTS OF THE COMPOUND OINTMENT

The Old Testament gives us the pictures, whereas the New Testament gives us the definition and description of these pictures. Let us consider the picture of the ingredients of the compound ointment in Exodus 30. The olive oil is the base, and it is mixed, blended, and compounded with four spices: myrrh, cinnamon, calamus, and cassia.

Olive Oil

Olive oil, according to typology, signifies the Spirit of God (Isa. 61:1; Heb. 1:9).

Myrrh

All good Bible students and teachers recognize that myrrh is a type of the death of Christ with all the sufferings which Christ passed through in His death. When Nicodemus helped to bury Jesus, he buried Him with myrrh and aloes (John 19:39).

Myrrh comes from an aromatic tree. This tree drops its juice either as the result of being cut or through some kind of natural opening or incision. It smells sweet but tastes bitter. Today we smell Christ's death, but He tasted death. Christ tasted death for us and its taste was bitter, but to us His death smells sweet. Myrrh signifies the suffering death of Christ.

Cinnamon

Fragrant cinnamon is extracted from the inner part of the bark of a certain tree. It not only has a distinctive flavor but also can be used to stimulate a weak heart. Cinnamon signifies the sweetness and effectiveness of Christ's death, which is so effective in healing us.

Calamus

The third spice is calamus. Calamus is a reed which grows and rises up out of a marsh or a muddy place. Even though it grows in a marsh, it is able to shoot up into the air. Calamus signifies the rising up, the resurrection, of Christ.

Cassia

The fourth spice is cassia. Cinnamon is from the inner part of the bark, and cassia is from the outer part. It is also a sweet and fragrant spice. In ancient times cassia was used as a repellent to drive away insects and snakes. Thus, it signifies the power, the effectiveness, of Christ's resurrection.

These four spices were added into the olive oil. Therefore, the death of Christ with its sweetness and effectiveness and the resurrection of Christ with its power were added to and compounded with the Spirit of God.

THE SIGNIFICANCE OF THE NUMBERS
RELATED TO THE COMPOUND OINTMENT

Now we need to consider the numbers related to the ingredients of the compound ointment. According to typology, all the numbers in the Bible are meaningful.

Humanity and Divinity
Compounded in the Spirit of God

There are four spices, and the number four in the Bible is the number of the creatures. The book of Ezekiel speaks of the four living creatures (1:5). Thus, the number four signifies humanity in God's creation. There were 500 shekels of myrrh, 250 shekels of cinnamon, 250 shekels of calamus, and 500 shekels of cassia in the compound ointment, giving a total of three units of 500 shekels each. The number three signifies the Triune God. From these numbers we can see that both humanity and divinity are compounded in the Spirit of God, the heavenly olive oil.

The Second of the Divine Trinity
Split on the Cross

Notice that the second unit of 500 shekels is split in half into two units of 250 shekels each. This signifies that the Second of the Divine Trinity was split through His death on the cross.

The Connection of Christ's Death and Resurrection

The two units of 250 shekels each are not complete. One signifies the sweetness and effectiveness of the Lord's death; the other signifies the precious resurrection of Christ. This shows that the Lord's death is incomplete. His resurrection must follow His death and be added to His death. These two things are not separate but are connected together.

The Complete, Perfect, Eternal, Divine Spirit

All of these elements are put into one hin of olive oil. This entire hin of olive oil signifies the complete, perfect, eternal, divine Spirit. The Spirit of God is complete and eternally perfect in Himself, but He still needs more ingredients to be consummated as the all-inclusive Spirit of Jesus Christ.

The Ability to Bear Responsibility

With the compound ointment, there is also the number five. The four spices plus the one hin of olive oil are five ingredients. In the Bible the number five signifies responsibility and the ability for bearing responsibility. Five is composed of four plus one. We may use the human hand as an illustration. On our hand we have four fingers and a thumb. Because of this our hand can do many things and bear responsibility.

In the Bible there are clear illustrations of the fact that five is the number of responsibility. The Ten Commandments were written on two tablets, five on each tablet. These five commandments on each tablet signify responsibility. Also, there are the ten virgins in Matthew 25. They are divided into two groups: five wise ones and five foolish ones. This shows that all the believers bear the responsibility of being filled with the Spirit.

We creatures are signified by the number four, and God is signified by the number one. When God is added to us, we have the ability to bear responsibility. Once we were the number four, but we have had the unique God added to us. Now we are the number five. Being without God is like having four fingers without a thumb. Just as it is awkward not to have a thumb, it is more than awkward not to have God.

As we have seen, there are three units of five hundred shekels of the spices. Thus, there is three times five hundred, and five hundred is one hundred times five. This signifies that in this compound ointment there is the fullness of ability for bearing responsibility.

The Compound Ointment for God's Building

Five and three are the basic numbers in the compound ointment. As we have seen, three is the number of the Godhead, and there are three units of five hundred shekels in the ointment. The second unit of five hundred shekels is split in half, indicating that the Second of the Divine Trinity was split on the cross. In the compound ointment, there are four spices added to one hin of olive oil. Five is four plus one—the creature plus the Creator to be the ability to bear responsibility.

I would like us to read a few portions from the Bible to see more of the significance of the numbers five and three.

Let us first consider the dimensions of the ark, which Noah built, in Genesis 6. After God created everything, He intended to build up something. The first item of God's building was the ark of Noah. The ark is the seed of God's building, and the New Jerusalem is the harvest of God's building. From this seed the New Jerusalem grows out and grows up.

The numbers three and five are prevalent in the dimensions of the ark, the first item of God's building. Genesis 6:15 says, "And this is the fashion which thou shalt make it of: The length of the ark shall be three hundred cubits, the breadth of

it fifty cubits, and the height of it thirty cubits." Verse 16 says
that the ark was to be made with "lower, second, and third
stories." Here with the dimensions of the ark, we have multi-
ples of the numbers three and five. Three, the number of
the Triune God, and five, the number of responsibility, the
number of God added to man, are the numbers of God's
building.

The dimensions of the tabernacle are also full of the
numbers three and five. As an example of this, Exodus 27:1
speaks of the dimensions of its altar: "And thou shalt make
an altar of shittim wood, five cubits long, and five cubits
broad; the altar shall be foursquare: and the height thereof
shall be three cubits." Again we see the numbers five and
three because they are the numbers of God's building.

Now let us read Exodus 25:10 concerning the dimensions
of the ark in the Holy of Holies: "And they shall make an
ark of shittim wood: two cubits and a half shall be the length
thereof, and a cubit and a half the breadth thereof, and a
cubit and a half the height thereof." Two and a half is half
of five, and one and a half is half of three. The altar is five
by three, and the ark is two and a half by one and a half.
The altar is a complete unit, but the ark is half the size of the
altar. The ark typifies Christ, and Christ has been split.
The "halved" Christ is the crucified Christ for God's building.
Again we see the basic numbers of five and three for God's
building.

The tabernacle was of three sections: the outer court, the
Holy Place, and the Holy of Holies. According to Exodus 27:13,
the width of the outer court on the east side was to be fifty
cubits. Then verses 14 and 15 say that the hangings on either
side of the gate were to be fifteen cubits with three pillars
and three sockets. Furthermore, verse 18 says that the height
of the linen curtains of the outer court was to be five cubits.
Actually, each curtain of the enclosure in the outer court
measured five cubits by five cubits.

The above illustrations should prove to us that the numbers three and five are the numbers for God's building.
This also shows us that the compound ointment is for God's
building. God charged Moses to anoint the tabernacle and

all the utensils of the tabernacle with this ointment (Exo. 30:26-29). Moses also was to anoint Aaron and his sons with the compound ointment (v. 30). This means that the all-inclusive Spirit is also for God's priesthood. If the tabernacle with everything related to it had not been anointed with the ointment, it would have been a secular building, not a holy building, not God's building. The tabernacle could never have been a divine building until every part of it was anointed with the holy compound ointment.

BUILDING UP THE CHURCH
BY THE ANOINTING OF THE COMPOUND SPIRIT

Do not think that I am burdened here to give a sermon on typology. My intention is to show us how we can have the church life. We can have the church life by being anointed with the compound Spirit. In 1 Corinthians there are the gifts, but 2 Corinthians speaks of the anointing. The building of God is established and built up by the anointing of the compound ointment, the compound Spirit.

Psalm 133 says, "Behold, how good and how pleasant it is for brethren to dwell together in unity! It is like the precious ointment..." (vv. 1-2a, KJV). The ointment is the unity, the oneness. This is why Ephesians 4:3 speaks of the oneness of the Spirit. The Spirit as the compound ointment is not just the Spirit of God, possessing merely divinity; the Spirit as the ointment has been compounded with Christ's divine and human natures, His death and its effectiveness, and His resurrection and its power.

Teachings and gifts alone cannot build up the church. The church, the Body of Christ, has been divided by teachings and gifts. Only the anointing of the Spirit of Jesus Christ as the compound ointment can build up the church. God is anointing us today with such an all-inclusive Spirit. In this ointment there is the effectiveness of Christ's death to kill all the divisive germs and negative things within our being.

THE SPIRIT OF THE GLORIFIED JESUS

Now I would like to quote a portion of Andrew Murray's masterpiece The Spirit of Christ. The following excerpts are taken from chapter five, which is entitled, "The Spirit of the Glorified Jesus."

We know how the Son, who had from eternity been with the Father, entered upon a new stage of existence when He became flesh. When He returned to Heaven, He was still the same only-begotten Son of God, and yet not altogether the same. For He was now also, as Son of Man, the first-begotten from the dead, clothed with that glorified humanity which He had perfected and sanctified for Himself. And just so the Spirit of God as poured out at Pentecost was indeed something new....When poured out at Pentecost, He came as the Spirit of the glorified Jesus, the Spirit of the Incarnate, crucified, and exalted Christ, the bearer and communicator to us, not of the life of God as such, but of that life as it had been interwoven into human nature in the person of Christ Jesus.

...From His nature, as it was glorified in the resurrection and ascension, His Spirit came forth as the Spirit of His human life, glorified into the union with the Divine, to make us partakers of all that He had personally wrought out and acquired, of Himself and His glorified life....And in virtue of His having perfected in Himself a new holy human nature on our behalf, He could now communicate what previously had no existence—a life at once human and Divine.

...And the Holy Spirit could come down as the Spirit of the God-man—most really the Spirit of God, and yet as truly the spirit of man.

Andrew Murray's teaching shows that today the Spirit of God is the Spirit of the glorified Jesus. He is the Spirit not merely with divinity but the Spirit both of God and of man with a renewed, uplifted, developed, new holy human nature. We are under the anointing of such a wonderful Spirit for the building up of the church as the Body of Christ.

CHAPTER ELEVEN

THE EXPERIENCE OF THE ANOINTING FOR THE CHURCH LIFE

Scripture Reading: Exo. 30:23-33; 2 Cor. 1:21-22

We want to have more fellowship concerning how we can grow so that the church might be built up. The way is by the anointing of the compound Spirit, typified by the compound ointment in Exodus 30.

BEING SANCTIFIED BY THE ANOINTING

We have seen that all the parts of the tabernacle with all its contents were not holy until they were anointed (Exo. 30:26-29). The anointing was the factor that made the entire tabernacle holy. This anointing sanctified the whole dwelling place of God. The word *sanctify* means to join something with God, to make something have the divine essence and nature of God.

To be sanctified is not to be sinlessly perfect, nor is it to be merely separated and changed in our position. Strictly speaking, to be sanctified means to be joined to God. Of course, if we are joined to God, we are separated. But this attachment to God is not only a change in position but also a change in disposition. By being sanctified our whole being is mingled with the divine, holy essence and transformed.

Romans 1:4 speaks of "the Spirit of holiness." Wuest's translation uses "divine essence" instead of "the Spirit of holiness." Thus, holiness is the divine essence of God's being. To be sanctified is to be joined, to be attached, to the divine essence. To be sanctified is to be made one with God and to make God one with us. This sanctification is carried out by the anointing Spirit, who anoints us with the divine essence of God.

We have seen from Exodus 30 that the compound ointment typifies the compound Spirit. The Spirit today is a compound. In the previous chapter, we saw all the ingredients of the compound ointment, which typify the ingredients of today's compound Spirit, who is anointing us all the time. The humanity and divinity of Christ, His death with its effectiveness, and His resurrection with its power have been compounded into the Spirit. The ability to bear responsibility and the building element are also elements of the compound Spirit. This is the bountiful Spirit of Jesus Christ (Phil. 1:19). All the elements of Christ's person and work have been put into this one Spirit, the compound Spirit.

All of the priests as well as the entire tabernacle with all of its parts were under the anointing of the compound ointment. Without this anointing, none of them could have been holy, that is, none of them could have been attached to God, joined to God. God's divine essence would have had nothing to do with any part of the tabernacle or with any one of the priests if they had not been anointed. This means that under the anointing of the compound Spirit, there is the dwelling place of God, the church life, the priesthood, and the real serving body.

We have to see that the Spirit is no longer the Spirit of God possessing merely divinity; the Spirit today is the Spirit of Jesus Christ, the compound Spirit typified by the compound ointment. The compound ointment in Exodus 30 is the holy anointing oil. To be holy is to be one with God. Regardless of how perfect you are, if you are not one with God and if God is not one with you, you are not holy.

What we need today in the church life is the anointing of the holy anointing oil, the compound Spirit. We can never build up a proper church life by teachings. Many years ago when people came to me with questions and problems, I was able to give them an answer. Today I have only one thing to say: "Go to the Lord and ask Him." Many years ago I taught people how to take care of their children, but that teaching did not work. Teaching does not work. If you teach me to be humble again and again, I can never be humble. The more teaching I get about being humble, the prouder I will become.

I could give you the best teaching on how we need to love one another, but eventually we will argue with one another. Teaching stirs up the thinking of the mentality, the exercise of the mind. It does not minister life to people. What we need today is not teaching but the anointing.

Every part of the tabernacle had to be anointed. It would have been foolish to teach the parts of the tabernacle to be holy. They did not need teaching to be holy. They needed something to make them holy. As the New Testament dwelling place of God, we also need something to make us holy—the compound Spirit. Do not teach me; instead, pour the compound Spirit upon me. Then even though I may not know the teaching of holiness, I am really holy. What we need is the reality, not the empty teaching. We need the reality of brotherly love, not the teaching. We need the essence of love, not the mere terminology of love. What we need today is to be anointed with God's essence by the anointing of the compound Spirit.

BEING ANOINTED WITH THE COMPOUND SPIRIT
BY CALLING ON THE NAME OF THE LORD

The book of Romans speaks of sanctification, transformation, conformation, and glorification. All of these are carried out by the anointing of the Spirit, and the Spirit is Christ Himself (2 Cor. 3:17). Some may ask, "Where is Christ?" Romans 10 says that there is no need to go to the heavens to bring Christ down or to go to the abyss to bring Christ up (vv. 6-7). Christ as the word is in our mouth (v. 8). He has become the living word, the Spirit, to be in our mouth like the air, the breath, that can be taken into our being. Christ today is the compound air, the life-giving Spirit, and we have to breathe Him in.

Romans 10 tells us the way to breathe Him in, that is, by calling on the name of the Lord. Verse 12 says that He is rich to all who call upon Him. In order to participate in the Lord's riches, we have to call upon Him day and night.

According to the priestly service in the tabernacle, the priests had to light the lamp and then burn the incense (Exo. 30:7). The lamp signifies the Word (Psa. 119:105), and the incense signifies prayer (Psa. 141:2). Whenever we come to light the lamp, we have to offer the incense. This shows that whenever we touch the Word, we have to pray. Praying should never be separated from dealing with the Word. Dealing with the Word needs the real praying. To light the lamp, you need to burn the incense.

The simplest way to pray is to call upon the name of the Lord. When we call on the name of the Lord, we get His person, and His person is the compound Spirit with all the ingredients of Christ's being and work. If we mingle our reading of the Word with calling on the Lord's name in prayer, we will be anointed with the compound Spirit, and spontaneously we will become holy.

Today what we need is not the teachings but the anointing. Every part of the church life needs to be anointed. This is why we have to call on the name of the Lord. The more we call on the name of the Lord, the more we are anointed with Him as the compound Spirit. Under this anointing we have the reality of the tent of meeting, the tabernacle, and the priesthood.

We have to turn away from the doctrinal teachings and cleave ourselves to calling upon the name of the Lord that we may be anointed. We have to be renewed and revolutionized. The anointing is always fresh, but the teachings are always old. We need to be freshly anointed with the Spirit continually by calling on the name of the Lord all day.

By this anointing we are sealed with the Spirit (2 Cor. 1:22). Actually, the anointing is the sealing. The seal is a mark that marks us out as God's inheritance. How can people realize that we are people of God? It is only by the anointing, the sealing, of the compound Spirit. When we are under the continual anointing and sealing of the Spirit, we give others the impression that we are the people of God, that we belong to God. If you dye a white shirt again and again with blue dye, eventually everyone is clear that it is a blue shirt. Similarly, if we are anointed with the Spirit continually, everyone will be clear that we belong to God, because we will be His expression. How can we know that we are saved? The more we are anointed, the more we are sure that we are saved. We doubt our salvation because we have not been anointed that much. The more we are anointed, the more we have the mark of the Spirit as the living seal, causing us to bear God's image.

Furthermore, the more we are anointed, the more we receive the pledge, the guarantee, the enjoyment, the foretaste, of the Spirit (2 Cor. 1:22). When we enter into eternity in the New Jerusalem, we will completely and eternally enjoy the compound Spirit. Today we have the pledge, the guarantee, the foretaste, of this Spirit.

If we are going to have a proper church life, to be built up together, and to serve the Lord as the priesthood, we need the anointing. Every part of the church life and everyone in the church life has to be anointed. We cannot have the building or the priesthood without being anointed. When we are under the anointing of the compound Spirit, we have the priesthood and the service in the Body. The way to be anointed is to call upon the name of the Lord continuously. The result is the building up of the tent of meeting, the dwelling place of God, and the priesthood in today's church life.

CHAPTER TWELVE

THE ANOINTING FOR TRANSFORMATION

Scripture Reading: 2 Cor. 1:21-22; 3:3, 6, 8, 17-18

Thus far, we have seen that there are four lines in both 1 and 2 Corinthians. The four lines in 1 Corinthians are the lines of Christ, the spirit, the church, and the gifts. In 2 Corinthians the gifts are replaced by the ministry which is produced through sufferings. The lines of Christ, the spirit, and the church in 2 Corinthians are spoken of in a very deep and subjective way.

We want to continue our fellowship on the line of the spirit in 2 Corinthians, the line of the divine Spirit with the human spirit. We have pointed out that there are nine aspects of the wonderful, all-inclusive, divine Spirit in 2 Corinthians. He is the anointing Spirit, the sealing Spirit, the pledging Spirit, the writing Spirit, the life-giving Spirit, the ministering Spirit, the liberating Spirit, the transforming Spirit, and the transmitting Spirit. In chapter thirteen we see the communion, the fellowship, the transmitting, of the Holy Spirit. That is the conclusion of 2 Corinthians. In chapters one and three are the remaining eight aspects of the Spirit. In chapter one we see the anointing, sealing, and pledging aspects of the Spirit. In chapter three there are another five aspects: the writing, life-giving, Christ-ministering, liberating, and transforming aspects. No doubt, the apostle Paul wrote 2 Corinthians with the thought of these eight aspects of the deeper work of the all-inclusive Spirit. This is why they are placed at the first part of this book.

THE ANOINTING SPIRIT

The first of these eight aspects is the anointing (1:21), and the last is the transforming (3:18). We have seen that God anoints us, paints us, with the compound Spirit, a compound of all the ingredients and elements of Christ's person and work. This ointment is the best heavenly paint, full of the riches of the Godhead and full of the riches of the person, work, and attainments of Christ. The more we are anointed, painted, with the compound Spirit, the more the elements of Christ's person and work are dispensed into our being. These elements are the Triune God in His divinity, Christ's humanity, His wonderful death with its effectiveness, and His resurrection with its power. All of these elements are included in this heavenly paint, the compound Spirit. This painting, this anointing, brings all these elements into our being.

Eventually, the transforming Spirit transforms us into His image. This is God's goal, His intention. God anoints us, paints us, with Himself for the purpose of transforming us to make us the real sons of our Father with the image of the Father. The divine painting, the anointing, is for the transforming. The anointing brings in all the elements, and the transforming makes us exactly the same as the Son of God in life and nature, transforming us into His image from glory to glory even as from the Lord Spirit. The ointment, the compound Spirit, is the Lord Spirit. By Him and from Him we are being transformed into His image.

The Triune God with His divinity mingled with humanity and including His wonderful death and resurrection is today the compound ointment to anoint us with all that He is and all that He has done so that we might be transformed into His image, and this transformation is from the Lord Spirit. We are being anointed, and eventually we will be transformed. I hope that the churches will pay more attention to this matter of anointing for transformation.

The more doctrinal teaching we receive, the more knowledge and concepts we gain; but the anointing brings in the substantial, real elements of Christ into our being. If I paint you with paint, you may not understand it, but you still are painted. Teaching brings in vain knowledge, but the anointing brings in the real substance.

We may be taught much about the death of Christ, but what we need is the substance and reality of the death of

Christ itself. His death is in the all-inclusive, compound Spirit. When I was young, I was taught about the death of Christ in Romans 6 and that we had to reckon ourselves as being dead (v. 11). But this is just the teaching of the death of Christ, not the reality. The reality of the death of Christ is in the Spirit, spoken of in Romans 8.

When we call on the name of the Lord, we receive the riches of the all-inclusive Spirit (Rom. 10:12). When we are about to lose our temper, we can call on the Lord's name, and the killing power of Christ's death is there to kill our temper. But the more that we try to reckon ourselves dead, the more we will be defeated, because this reckoning is the exercise of the mind. When we forget about the exercise of the mind and exercise our spirit by calling on the name of the Lord, we touch the compound Spirit. In this compound Spirit, there is the divine germicide to kill all the negative things in our being. The germ killing, the killing death of Christ, is not in the teaching but in the compound Spirit. The Christian life is not a matter of knowing doctrines but a matter of being anointed by the compound Spirit.

THE SEALING SPIRIT

In between the anointing and the transforming, there are another six aspects of the Spirit: the sealing, the pledging, the writing, the life-giving, the Christ-ministering, and the liberating. The anointing becomes the sealing within us (2 Cor. 1:22), giving us the mark and the impression of the image of God to show that we belong to God.

THE PLEDGING SPIRIT

The seal of the Spirit, which is constituted with the elements brought in by the anointing, becomes the pledge, the guarantee, the down payment, the foretaste, of the Spirit (v. 22). This means that we have the Spirit for our taste, our enjoyment. The Christian life is not a matter of meditating in the mind but a matter of tasting the Lord in the spirit (Psa. 34:8; 1 Pet. 2:3). We can taste the heavenly things and the things of the age to come (Heb. 6:4-5) by the transmitting Spirit. He also transmits the things in eternity and in the

New Jerusalem to us because He is the eternal Spirit (Heb. 9:14).

He transmits all the heavenly things and elements of Christ into us not for our mental knowledge but for us to taste, to enjoy. We need to be those who are continually tasting the heavenly, spiritual, eternal things by the compound Spirit. Everything in the New Jerusalem is included in the compound Spirit, who has been given to us as a foretaste, a sample, of the full taste of the Spirit in the ages to come. The quantity of the Spirit we have in this age might be smaller, but the quality and the taste are the same. We have to learn how to taste the Lord by continually calling upon His name.

We can never be humble by being taught to be humble. Actually, the more we are taught to be humble, the prouder we will become. If we are taught to love others, eventually we will not love anyone. The real love and the real essence of love are in the compound Spirit. God is love (1 John 4:8), and He is the compound Spirit today. The more we touch the compound Spirit, the more the essence of love will get into us. There is no need for us to learn to love others. When we are infused with the essence of love in the compound Spirit, we will spontaneously love others.

Love is the essence of the divine life. A carnation flower does not bloom by being taught, but by its growth out of its life essence. The more the flower grows, the more it expresses its life essence. Likewise, the more we grow in the divine life, the more we express the essence of the divine life. We cannot be holy, spiritual, and heavenly by being taught. Eventually, we will become worldly. The heavenly essence is not in any teaching, but in the compound Spirit.

In 2 Corinthians 1:21 the apostle Paul said that God was the One who "firmly attaches us with you unto Christ and has anointed us." We need to consider why the apostle Paul said this. When he wrote 2 Corinthians, the Corinthian believers were doubting his apostolic authority. Some even claimed that he was an insincere, fickle person, a man of yes and no. This is why he told them that the Christ he preached to them was always yes (1:19-20). Then he told the Corinthians that he was a real priest in the priesthood who had been anointed by God. In ancient times no one could assume the position and function of a priest unless he had been anointed. Paul said that he was anointed and attached to the Head of the priesthood, Christ, the anointed One.

After the compounding of the ointment in Exodus 30, God told Moses to anoint all the parts of the tabernacle and Aaron and his sons (vv. 26-30). Aaron became the anointed one, and all his sons were attached to him. Then all his sons were anointed. The apostle Paul used this background to indicate to the Corinthians that today Christ is our real Aaron. He is the High Priest, and we are His sons. God has attached us to Him, and God has anointed us. We are assuming the position and function of priests because we have been attached to Christ, the anointed One.

God has anointed and appointed Christ to be the Head of the priesthood, and we all have been attached to Him. Thus, we are the sons of the real Aaron today. We have become the priests of the divine priesthood because we have been attached to the Head Priest, and we have been anointed by God. Paul's proof of his apostleship was the anointing. He was attached to Christ, the anointed One, and he was anointed by God. When the priests were anointed, they were consecrated and commissioned.

This ointment became Paul's seal, sealing him to assume his priestly position. The Spirit sealed him with everything of Christ's person, work, and attainments. These elements of Christ upon him were his seal to prove that he was anointed by God to serve Him as a priest. Furthermore, this anointing and sealing became a foretaste to Paul. No matter what the Corinthians thought of Paul, he testified that he was enjoying the Spirit as a foretaste. The anointing and the sealing brought him the divine element for him to enjoy.

I want to say again that what we need today is not doctrinal teaching, but the heavenly anointing with the heavenly ointment. We are consecrated, commissioned, ordained, and inaugurated into our priesthood by being anointed. The anointing is the painting of all that Christ is, all that He has done, and all that He has attained into our being. We have been firmly attached to God's anointed One, and we have been anointed. This anointing is the sealing, and this seal becomes the foretaste, the pledge, for our enjoyment.

THE WRITING SPIRIT

Paul went on to tell the Corinthians that they were the letters of Christ who had been inscribed by the apostles with the Spirit of the living God as the divine, heavenly ink (3:3). The Spirit is neither the writer nor the pen but the writing ink to write Christ into our being. The more we are written on with the Spirit, the more of the heavenly ink we have. This writing is like the anointing, the painting. The Spirit as the ink brings the heavenly element into us to make this element one with us.

Paul was anointed, so he was an apostle; the Corinthians had been inscribed with the Spirit, so they were the letters. Without being anointed, he could not have been an apostle. Without being inscribed with the Spirit as the ink, they could not have been letters. To anoint is with ointment; to write is with ink. Actually, the ointment is the ink. The ingredients and the elements within the ink are the same as those within the ointment.

Writing brings ink to the paper; it does not correct the paper. The Spirit is the ink, and the content of the ink is Christ with His person, work, and attainments. This heavenly ink is a compound of all the elements of Christ. The more we are inscribed with this ink, the more we have the elements of Christ dispensed into us. Then we become a letter of Christ with Christ as our content.

The more I write on a piece of paper, the more the essence of ink saturates the paper. The Spirit as the compound ink adds the substance of Christ into us and saturates us with the essence of Christ. Then we have the substance of Christ to really express Christ. There may not be much of Christ in our mind, emotion, and will. But when we are written on with the Spirit again and again, the essence of Christ is dispensed into us. Then our mind, emotion, and will express Christ because Christ has been inscribed into these parts of our soul. The essence and elements of Christ are added into us by the writing of the heavenly ink, the compound Spirit.

THE LIFE-GIVING SPIRIT

Next Paul spoke of the life-giving Spirit (3:6). The Spirit does not give knowledge but life. While we are being written on with the heavenly ink, the compound Spirit, this Spirit imparts life to us. The more ink we get, the more life we get, and the more the essence of Christ is added to us. Then we have the real growth in life. The more we are written on with the heavenly compound Spirit, the more we receive the essence of the life of Christ. This life is real, living, strengthening, energizing, satisfying, and fruit-bearing. The writing Spirit is the life-giving Spirit. He writes on us by imparting life into us.

THE MINISTERING SPIRIT

This Spirit is also the ministering Spirit (3:8). He ministers Christ into us. Then He ministers Christ to others through us.

THE LIBERATING SPIRIT

This ministering Spirit is the liberating Spirit (v. 17), who breaks all the bonds, takes away the veils, and releases us. The essence of Christ must be dispensed into us to liberate us.

THE TRANSFORMING SPIRIT

Eventually, this all-inclusive Spirit is the transforming Spirit (v. 18). He transforms us, not by correcting or adjusting us, but by putting more and more of the life essence of Christ into us. We have the life power of Christ to shape us with His life essence so that we can be shaped into His life form. As an illustration, the life power of the peach life shapes the peach with its life essence to produce the form of a peach. We are being transformed and conformed into Christ's glorious image from glory to glory by the Lord Spirit.

I want to emphasize the fact that we *are being* transformed. We are as mirrors beholding and reflecting the Lord to be transformed into His image from glory to glory. When a carnation comes into full blossom, that is its glory. One day we will come into full blossom, and that will be the glorification and manifestation of the sons of God. That will be a glorious liberty, the liberty of glory. The entire creation is groaning and waiting for that liberty (Rom. 8:19-22). That freedom of the manifestation and glorification of the sons of God will be the consummation of our transformation.

Praise the Lord that we are now in the process of being transformed. We should not try to outwardly adjust or improve ourselves. Instead, we need to be anointed and sealed with the Spirit. We need to enjoy the Spirit as the foretaste. We need to be inscribed with the Spirit and enjoy His life-giving power. Finally, we need to experience the ministry of the Spirit and enjoy Him as the liberating and transforming One. The more we read the word prayerfully and call upon the name of the Lord, the more we will enjoy the compound Spirit so that we can be transformed and conformed to the Lord's glorious image.

CHAPTER THIRTEEN

THE HUMAN SPIRIT
IN SECOND CORINTHIANS

Scripture Reading: 2 Cor. 2:13; 4:13, 16; 6:6; 7:1, 13; 12:18

In this chapter we want to see the revelation concerning the human spirit in 2 Corinthians. Second Corinthians covers not only the Holy Spirit of God but also the human spirit. Paul covers the human spirit not in the way of doctrinal teaching but in the way of experience. He did not teach doctrinally about the human spirit, but from his writing we can see that he was a person always living, acting, and walking in his spirit. Second Corinthians may be considered as an autobiography of the apostle Paul. In this autobiography we see that he always acted in his spirit. First Corinthians speaks about the human spirit, but the second Epistle speaks about the human spirit in a deeper way.

THE REST IN OUR SPIRIT

In 2 Corinthians 2:12-13 Paul said, "Furthermore, when I came to Troas for the gospel of Christ and a door was open to me in the Lord, I had no rest in my spirit, for I did not find Titus my brother; but taking leave of them, I went forth into Macedonia." If we were composing this portion, we might say, "When I came to Los Angeles to visit some of my worldly friends, and the door of the gospel was shut to me by the Lord, I had no rest in my spirit." But Paul did not say this. He said that he came to Troas to preach the gospel of Christ and that the door was opened to him by the Lord. But he did not have the rest in his spirit, so he went away.

Since the Lord opened the door, why did Paul leave? Are we going to follow what the Lord has done, or are we going to follow what we feel in our spirit? It seems that since a door was open to Paul in the Lord, this must have been the Lord's will. Some were taught that although the door was opened to Paul of the Lord, he gave in to his own personal weakness, because his brother Titus was not there. We may think that Paul was too selfish and that he just cared for his feeling and not for the Lord's interest.

Now let us consider whether Paul's leaving was right or wrong. We need to realize that the apostle Paul was absolutely right because he was very subjective, not objective. He did not care for the outward situation. What he cared for was the inward feeling. Now I would like to ask, "Was the Lord more intimate with Paul in the open door or in Paul's spirit?" The door was opened by the Lord, but the Lord was more intimate to Paul in his spirit. Here we all have to learn a lesson. This lesson is that we should not care too much about the outward circumstances. Even if there is a door opened by the Lord to us, if we just care for this and not for the Lord Himself in our spirit, we are not very intimate with the Lord.

We can illustrate this by a parent's relationship with his or her child. Sometimes the parent would tell the child that it is all right for him to do something, but the child may sense that he will lose the intimacy of his parent if he does that certain thing. In our service to the Lord, He may open a door for us to go on, yet we may feel deep within that we have no rest. Do we want the open door or the rest in our spirit? I can testify that a number of times the Lord opened the door widely to me, but I did not have the rest. I could not go through the door; I had to go along with the rest. The inner rest is the green light, not the open door.

In a sense this is a difficult walk, but it is a closer walk in the Lord. It is a walk of intimacy with the Lord. Some may say that they have a door widely opened to them in the mission field, but do they have the rest within? We may take the door and drop the rest. We may go somewhere and do a great work, but not have the rest within. Do we want the door or the rest? The door is in verse 12, and the rest is in verse 13. The apostle Paul was not the same as many Christians are today in their service. They just care for the door. But do we have the rest in our spirit? Would we sacrifice the door for the rest?

Paul paid the price to take care of the rest in his spirit. Even though the Lord opened the door to him, he sacrificed that door. He paid that price to keep the rest. This shows that we should take care of the inner rest all the time. If we just take care of the outward situation, environment, and circumstances, we are through with the Lord. We must learn to restrict ourselves to the inner feeling. The outward situation may be favorable to us, but we should not care for that. We should care for just one thing—the inner rest.

If we do not have the rest in our spirit, how can the Lord have rest with us? Many times the Lord would allow us to have a choice. We should say, "Lord, my choice is not Your work or the doors opened by You. My choice is just You." The Lord may allow us to go through the open door, but if we do, we will lose the rest. The Lord may open the door for us to preach, but if we go through the door, we will lose the rest. This is a deep lesson for us to learn. We should not care much for the outward situation. Even if the outward circumstances are in favor of us, that still is not the green light. The green light is only the inner rest.

Rest includes the thought of relief, peace, and ease. If you have no rest, this means that you have no relief, peace, or ease. You may say that it is right for you to stay in a certain place to do a work for the Lord, but deep within you may have no relief, peace, or ease. Others may not know this, but you do. You may argue that the door has been opened by the Lord for you, but you still have an inner strain and feel bound within. Your arguing in a vindicating way is according to the consideration in your mind, not according to the registration in your spirit. We need to take care of the inner relief, peace, and ease within our spirit. This is one basic, spiritual principle in the matter of life. If we are going to grow in life, we should not care for the outward circumstances. We have to take care of the inner feeling of whether or not we have the rest deep within us.

The inner anointing has much to do with this inner feeling of rest. A sister once gave a testimony of how she had been given a certain amount of money. She went to the department store, where she saw a piece of wool on sale. The more she considered the cheap price and the money the Lord had sent her, the more she was convinced that she was right to buy that piece of wool. But at the same time, she did not have the peace. Still, after much consideration she bought it. Later she came to a meeting and gave this testimony. She said that after she bought that piece of wool, she could not pray. She felt bound in the spirit because she had lost the inner peace, rest, and ease. What she had done was not sinful. But she lost the peace until she sold that piece of wool to someone else. Then the peace came back.

Have we learned the lesson to take care of the inner peace and not the outward circumstances? Paul had a door opened to him by the Lord to preach the gospel. This was something very good, not sinful. But he did not have the rest. What we do is not a matter of argument, but a matter of the inner rest. In the heavenly court, the more you argue, the more you lose. The Lord might say to us, "My child, I know that your circumstances and reasons are good, but do you have the rest with the Lord? Do you care for the outward circumstances or the inward rest? I am not in the outward circumstances. I am in your spirit."

A wife may say that she is right in her argument with her husband. She may be right, but does she have the peace? Sometimes the brothers may complain about their wives, but do they have the rest? Would we go along with being right in our complaint, or would we go along with the rest? To follow the rest you have to pay a price. To argue may give you a certain kind of pleasure, but you lose the Lord's presence; you do not have the rest with the Lord. I am not speaking of the rest in your thinking or of the satisfaction in your emotion. I am speaking of the real ease, relief, peace, and rest in your spirit. We all have to learn this deeper lesson. I encourage you all to follow the Lord in this way. This is the way to grow in life. Never care for the outward circumstances; always care for the inner rest.

THE SPIRIT OF FAITH

In 2 Corinthians 4:13 Paul said, "And having the same spirit of faith according to that which is written, 'I believed,

therefore I spoke,' we also believe, therefore we also speak."
This verse says that we have the spirit of faith, so we speak.
We speak, not according to our mind, not according to what we
think, but according to what is written. We do not speak in
the meetings, because we are so much in the mind. When we
are in the mind, we have a mind of doubts, not a spirit of
faith. Doubts are in our mind, but faith is in our spirit. If we
turn from our mind to our spirit, we have faith. If we turn
back to our mind, we have doubts.

When you are in the meeting, you may agree with everything that is said, but after you go back home, you may turn
to your mind and begin to doubt what you heard. The book of
Genesis tells us that Satan did his best to turn Eve from her
spirit to her mind (3:1-5). When he succeeded in this, Eve had
a question mark put in her concerning God. Faith is in the
spirit. When you turn to the spirit, you believe.

This believing faith immediately becomes the speaking
faith. When we believe, we will speak. To talk is one thing, but
to speak is another thing. We come to the meeting to speak,
not to talk. The Scripture says, "I believed, therefore I spoke."
It should be the same with us.

Many of you do not open up your mouth in the meeting,
because even after you come through the entrance into the
meeting hall, you are still in your mind. When you look at
yourself and at the other brothers and sisters, you have a
lot of considerations. As the saints are functioning in the
meeting, you may say to yourself things like this: "This one
is too poor." "This one is too loud." "That is a word without
experience." "That is shouting without reality." When you are
thinking in this way, you are in your mind, so your mouth
is shut up by your thinking. The more you think, the more
you consider, the harder it is for you to open up your mouth.
You do not speak, because you are so much in the mind. You
need the spirit of faith. You need to turn yourself to the
spirit.

Sometimes when you come into the meeting, you may have
a sensation that the atmosphere is dull. Actually, this sensation of dullness is Satan himself. This is his subtlety to defeat
you. When you have this sensation, you should immediately

declare that Satan is a liar. Then you should open up your mouth to speak for the Lord. If you practice this, the meetings will be in the third heaven.

A brother may call a hymn, and for no reason you will think that you do not like that hymn. That is the subtlety of the enemy. You have to overcome this. You should say, "I believe. I turn to the spirit of faith." If you remain in the mind, Satan has many ways to catch you. If you turn to the spirit, you will not care about what hymn has been called. Nothing will bother you.

A number of the saints are fragile; they are easily subdued and broken. They will be depressed by just a little thing. We all must learn to turn ourselves to the spirit. When we turn to the spirit, we have the spirit of faith. Then we will speak. Sometimes when I come to the meeting to minister, frustrating things will come up one by one. Even when I come into the entrance of the meeting hall, something might happen. This is the work of Satan. I have learned the lesson not to care for all these disturbing things. I have the spirit of faith, and I must speak in the spirit of faith. I do not care for all the troubling, outward circumstances. But many of us fluctuate too much simply because we are not so stable in the spirit. We have to learn the lesson to stay in the spirit. Do not care for the mind. Stay in the spirit. Then you will have the faith and the speaking spirit.

THE INNER MAN

Second Corinthians 4:16 speaks of the outer man and the inner man. The outer man needs to be consumed. This consuming takes place gradually, little by little. I have been under this consuming for many years, and my outer man still has not been thoroughly consumed. If we are going to live and act in our spirit, the outer man needs to be consumed all the time. Then the inner man is being renewed day by day. Our outer man needs to be reduced, not corrected, and our inner man needs to be renewed. Renewal is a matter of life. We need to be metabolically renewed day by day with the fresh supply of the resurrection life.

We are old because we remain in the soul so much. As long

as we remain in the soul, we are old. We need to be transferred from the soul to the spirit, and this transfer is the
renewing. To be renewed day by day simply means to be
transferred all the time from the soul to the spirit. This is not
a matter of teaching. Teaching does not work. This is absolutely a matter in life. We should always learn to turn from
the outer man to the inner man.

A HOLY SPIRIT

In 2 Corinthians 6 Paul said that he and his co-workers
commended themselves as ministers of God "in a holy spirit"
(vv. 4, 6). This refers to their regenerated spirit. This means
that our spirit must be holy. Thus, in the next chapter Paul
said that we have to purify ourselves from all defilement of
the flesh and of the spirit (7:1). Then the spirit will be holy,
and we will perfect holiness in the fear of God. We need to
purify ourselves so that the holiness of God can saturate our
entire being.

We may be right in our reasoning and arguing, but we are
not holy in our spirit. We need a holy spirit without any
defilement, even without the defilement of arguments. We
may be right in our mind, in our soul, in our argument, but
filthy in our spirit. The more we talk and argue, the more we
are right, but the more we are defiled in our spirit. We may be
right in our doing, but not so holy in our spirit. We need a holy
spirit, a spirit separated from all things unto God. We need
a spirit that does not care for anything except God Himself.
Then we get rid of all the defilements, such as arguments and
reasonings.

We may have many reasons, but all those reasons are
filthy to our spirit. We can be defiled in our spirit not just
with outwardly sinful things but with something which
is right, but other than God. Anything other than God is a
defilement to our spirit. We need to be separated and consecrated to the Lord inwardly. Our spirit must be solely and
wholly separated unto God. If our spirit is tied to anything other than God, that becomes a defilement. We need a
holy spirit.

REFRESHED IN OUR SPIRIT

In 2 Corinthians 7:13 Paul said, "We rejoiced more abundantly over the joy of Titus, because his spirit has been refreshed by all of you." Here we have a number of lessons to learn.

First, you have to refresh others' spirits. Many times when you are with a certain brother or sister, after a while you feel the refreshment in your spirit. Someone else may be able to make you happy in your emotion but not refreshed in your spirit. Sometimes your emotional feeling may be hurt, yet your spirit is refreshed. To make people happy in the emotion is one thing. To make people refreshed in the spirit is another thing. So we all have to learn the lesson of refreshing others' spirits.

Second, you also need to learn to be refreshed in your spirit. Sometimes you do not care for this refreshment in the spirit. Instead, you care for people's sympathy. If you are in a certain kind of trouble or trial, someone may sympathize with you and say something good to you. You may like this. But if someone would do something to refresh your spirit, you would not receive it. You have no willingness to have your spirit refreshed by someone. You have to learn to be refreshed in your spirit. You should not care for people's sympathizing with you or saying something good to you. You should care only for your spirit being refreshed by others.

Third, we have to learn to be joyful in others' refreshment. Paul was joyful in the refreshment of Titus's spirit. Some times we do not care for others' refreshment. We need to refresh others' spirits; we need to have our own spirit refreshed by others; and we need to be joyful in others' refreshment.

WALKING IN THE SAME SPIRIT

In 2 Corinthians 12:18 Paul said that he and Titus walked in the same spirit and in the same steps. The spirit here is our regenerated spirit indwelt by the Holy Spirit. This spirit governs, rules, directs, regulates, and leads us in our Christian walk (Rom. 8:4). The apostles walked in such a spirit. Paul did not say that they walked in the same doctrine, but in the same spirit. To walk includes speaking, thinking, talking, fellowshipping, and doing anything. We have to walk in the same spirit and in the same steps in a corporate way.

CHAPTER FOURTEEN

THE CHURCHES IN SECOND CORINTHIANS

Scripture Reading: 2 Cor. 1:1; 6:16; 8:1, 18-19, 23-24; 11:8, 28

As we have pointed out, 2 Corinthians is an improvement over the first book in the experience of Christ, in the spirit, and in the church. Furthermore, the gifts spoken of in the first book are replaced by the ministry in the second book. In this chapter we want to see the churches in 2 Corinthians.

OUR NEED TO IMPROVE BY KNOWING THE CHURCHES

We all must improve from knowing the church in a general way, or a so-called universal way, to knowing it in a local, specific, and practical way. Many Christians do not know anything about the church. Some Christians know something about the church, yet they know only about the universal church. But there is a small number of Christians who not only know the church but also know the local churches.

The universal church is more or less something in doctrine, in teaching, and in theory. But the churches are the practicality of the universal church. Many Christian teachers have spoken many messages and have written many expositions on the book of Ephesians regarding the church. Of all the expositions that have been written regarding the church, the majority are on Ephesians. But when we move from Ephesians to 2 Corinthians, we move from the church to the churches. There are very few expositions on the book of 2 Corinthians. The church, we may say, is the ABCs, while the churches are more advanced. Some have said that 2 Corinthians shows us the sufferings of the apostle Paul. This is true, but they do not see the reason that Paul suffered. Paul was suffering for the churches. You may have been taught about the church, but have you ever been taught about the churches? To know the churches is a great improvement. Some of us may know the church only in a doctrinal, general, weak, and even vague way. But we do not know the churches in a practical, particular, and specific way. We need to go on from knowing the church in Ephesians to knowing the churches in 2 Corinthians.

The word *churches,* in the plural number, is used many times in the book of 2 Corinthians. In Ephesians there is only the church in the singular number, not the churches. In 2 Corinthians 1:1, the church is mentioned in the singular number, but that is the church which is at Corinth, not in the universe. Besides this verse, all the references to the church in this book are in the plural number—churches. Verse 1 of chapter eight refers to the churches in Macedonia. Verse 18 of the same chapter mentions a brother who was praised in the gospel throughout all the churches, and verse 19 says that this brother was chosen by the churches. In verse 23 we read of the messengers, or apostles, of the churches, and in verse 24 the Corinthians were exhorted to show before the churches the proof of their love. In 11:8 Paul said that he robbed other churches, and in verse 28 that he bore anxiety for all the churches. He had many burdens that pressed upon him daily, and they were the care for all the churches. In 12:13 Paul asked the Corinthians if they were inferior to other churches. It is all the time the churches, not the church.

We cannot find one instance of the word *church* in 2 Corinthians in the sense of the universal church. There are altogether eight verses with the word *churches*. Have you ever noticed them? I venture to say that many have not. They have noticed the church, but not the churches. They have begun, but they have not advanced. Second Corinthians is not the beginning; it is the advance in the local churches.

Do not think that I am boasting or being critical. It is a fact that many Christians know the church but not the churches because they have not improved. It is abundantly clear in the Word that the churches are a step beyond the church. With the church we are in doctrine, in theory, but with the churches we come into the practice and reality. Many speak about the church as the Body of Christ, about the Body life and the Body ministry. Some speak of the New Testament church. But where is the reality of the local church life? Some even speak despitefully of the local church. If they are right, we had better remove 2 Corinthians from the New Testament. This book is full of the local churches.

Every truth in the Bible develops progressively, and the truth of the church is no exception. The church was first mentioned by the Lord Jesus in Matthew 16 (v. 18). That was the seed. But immediately after chapter sixteen, the Lord touched the local aspect of the church. In chapter sixteen there is the church, while in chapter eighteen there is the church in a locality, the church to which you can go. If you have some problem, you must "tell it to the church" (v. 17). Then in the book of Acts, we see the growing up of this seed into all the local churches—the church at Jerusalem (8:1), the church at Antioch (13:1), etc. Following this, in the Epistles there is the definition of the church. Finally, in 2 Corinthians and in Revelation, the local churches are strongly emphasized. The local churches are the harvest of the truth concerning the church.

With the teaching regarding this matter in the Bible, there is no ambiguity. It is exceedingly clear. By constant repetition and emphasis the Lord has driven this matter home. The final confirmation is in Revelation 1:11: "What you see write in a scroll and send it to the seven churches: to Ephesus and to Smyrna and to Pergamos and to Thyatira and to Sardis and to Philadelphia and to Laodicea." There are seven cities with seven churches—not seven churches in one city, but seven churches in seven cities. There should be one church in one city, and one city for one church. Nothing could be clearer.

THE PRACTICE OF THE CHURCH

The book of 1 Corinthians tells us something about the local church, but it is not very extensive, and it is mostly in the way of teaching. In 2 Corinthians, however, we do not have the teaching of the church, but the real practice of the church. We do need the teaching, but we cannot do without the practice. In certain high school and college courses, there is first a lecture and then a lab. The lab is where the lecture is put into practice, and it is certainly an improvement, practically speaking, upon the lecture. One is in theory, and the other is in practice. Let us see the practice of the church in the book of 2 Corinthians.

In 1:1 there is a compound subject—the apostle Paul and Timothy. It is not the apostle Paul *with* Brother Timothy, but the apostle Paul *and* Brother Timothy. They are writing unto the church of God which is at Corinth *with* all the saints. They did not write to the church *and* all the saints, but to the church *with* all the saints. The saints cannot be on the same level as the church. The saints belong to the church and are included in the church; therefore, the apostle used the word *with*. The saints are not the unit; only the church is the unit. It is not the church at Corinth *and* all the saints, but the church at Corinth *with* all the saints. Timothy could be on the same level as the apostle Paul, but the saints could not be on the same level as the church. You are not a unit; you are part of a unit. You belong to the church; the church is the unit. Second Corinthians is for the local church and for those in the local churches.

Beginning from chapter eight, all the references to the church are plural in number. Verse 1 of chapter eight says that the grace of God was given in the churches in Macedonia. Macedonia was a province of the Roman Empire, just as California is a state of the United States. In one province there were many churches. In the one state of California, there must also be many churches, such as the church in Los Angeles, the church in San Francisco, the church in Sacramento, etc. The churches in California are not the churches in Los Angeles, just as the churches in Macedonia were not the churches in Thessalonica, one of the cities of Macedonia. Corinth was a city belonging to Achaia, which was another province, south of Macedonia. In one city there could be one church; but in one province there must be many churches, because in one province there are many cities.

The grace of God given in the churches refers to the giving of material things. If we give something for the need of other saints or for the need of other churches, this is giving grace. Sometimes we think that as far as our giving is concerned, it has nothing to do with the church, but I am burdened to tell you that even this should be related to the church. It must not be an independent thing. By this we may realize how much the saints in the early days were possessed by the churches. They did not do their giving by themselves; they did it in the churches and through the churches.

In 8:18 we read of a brother whose praise in the gospel was throughout all the churches. Not only the church in one place would say that this brother was marvelous, but also all the churches. If you are praised by only one church, there may be a problem. The church in Los Angeles may praise you, but what about the church in San Francisco and the church in Sacramento? Your praise must be throughout all the churches. One church could be wrong, but it is hard for all the churches to be wrong. If all the churches say that a certain brother is not good, it certainly means that this brother is not good. If all the churches speak well of a certain brother, it is real proof that this brother is good in the Lord. It is not an individualistic matter; it is a real Body matter.

Verse 19 of this same chapter says that this brother was chosen by the churches. It is easy to be chosen by the Lord, for the Lord is the only one. But it is rather difficult to be chosen by the churches. Some church may like you, but some may not. Some may say amen to you, but some may not. Yet here it says that this brother was chosen by the churches. It is really a Body matter.

Brothers and sisters, have you seen such a thing on the earth today? Here is the improvement from the church to the churches. Yes, every local church has its own administration, but still the churches are one. What a beautiful and marvelous sight! This is a real improvement.

Some may say, "We are the church in Los Angeles. Let us alone. You are the church in San Francisco. Don't interfere with us; don't bother us." In a sense, each of the churches is local in its administration, but we need to realize that all the churches should be one. We are not unified or organized to be one, but if we mean business to practice the real church life, all the local churches will be one. There is no organization, no control, no center, yet the many local churches are one. This is indeed marvelous!

In 8:23 some brothers are spoken of as the apostles of the churches. This means that they are the ones sent by the churches, and they are the glory of Christ. It is not just a matter between you and the Lord, nor between you and your local church, but between you and the local churches. If you are sent out, it is not only by your local church but by the churches. All the churches agree in this one thing.

Then the apostle, in verse 24, advised the church in Corinth to show their love before all the churches. We are to show something for the Lord in the sight of all the churches. It is very practical. We do need a practical church life.

In 11:8 we see how frank and how absolutely unpolitical the apostle Paul was. He said, "I robbed other churches, taking wages for the ministry to you." I love the apostle Paul for his frankness. In 12:13 we see the same thing. He was so genuine. Brothers and sisters, in the church life we need to be genuine and frank. Do not think that this is a small matter. In the church life you cannot tell a brother to his face that he is good, and then behind his back say that he is not good. If there is no need to say anything, it is better not to say anything. Who are we to criticize? The Lord is the Judge. Whether brothers or sisters are right or wrong, the Lord knows. Leave this matter to the Lord. We must be wise and not say so many things criticizing this and that. But sometimes, as the leading ones, it is necessary to speak, not with the intent of criticizing, but with the burden of bearing responsibility. If I must say something about you, then whether in your presence or behind your back, I must speak according to the truth. We must learn the lesson of being genuine and frank. We must never say anything in two ways with two faces. If we say something, we must not speak loosely or lightly, but frankly in the presence of the Lord. Then we can have the church life.

If you are dealing with only one local church, it is comparatively easy to be two-faced and go undetected. But if more churches are involved, you will be exposed. How do you behave in Los Angeles, and how do you behave in San Francisco? If you are political, sooner or later you will be exposed. If you cannot be exposed in the first church, you will be exposed in the second. If not in the second, in the third or the fourth. Then your whole fabrication will collapse. The churches are the proving ground to us.

Finally, in 11:28 the apostle Paul said, "Apart from the things which have not been mentioned, there is this: the crowd of cares pressing upon me daily, the anxious concern for all the churches." How much the apostle Paul cared for the churches! It says here that he cared for all the churches, not for the church. How practical Paul was!

We all need to know the churches, not just the church. It is more than worthwhile to sell ourselves for the local churches. I am so happy that I have been spoiled for everything else by this. I do not have any taste for anything but the local churches. May the Lord be merciful to us that we may all be so clear and practical.

THE PROGRESSION OF THE LORD'S RECOVERY

In the Lord's recovery of the experience of the church life, there is a progression. In the last century, the Lord recovered the *doctrine* of the church through the Brethren. Then in the beginning of this century, the Lord recovered something more, that is, the spiritual principles, the *spirituality,* of the church. But this was still not so practical. Then after the year 1930, the Lord began to reveal the *practicality* of the church—not just the doctrine, not just the spirituality, but the practicality. The doctrine is certainly right and necessary. The spirituality is definitely right and necessary. The spirituality is definitely required and is even an improvement upon the doctrine. But in what way can we practice the church life? Must we wait until the New Jerusalem? No. The church life must be practiced today, and there is no other way but *the local churches.* Without the local churches, we cannot have the practical church life. There must be *the churches.*

It is interesting and regrettable to see how Christians in each stage of the Lord's recovery of the church life have criticized and opposed those in the succeeding one. Those

without the doctrine of the church criticized those who intro-
duced it. Then those with the doctrine of the church opposed
those who saw the spirituality of the church. Eventually,
those who see the spirituality of the church criticize the
matter of the practicality of the church. This is exactly the
situation.

May the Lord be merciful to us that we may be in the
forefront of His recovery.

CHAPTER FIFTEEN

MINISTRY PRODUCED THROUGH SUFFERING

Scripture Reading: 2 Cor. 1:4-6, 8-9; 4:8-12, 16-17; 6:3-5, 8-10; 11:23-28; 12:7-10

In this chapter we come to the last line of 2 Corinthians, that is, the line of the ministry produced through suffering. In the first book there are the gifts, but in the second book there is the ministry.

HOW THE MINISTRY IS PRODUCED

Both 1 and 2 Corinthians were written to the same church, yet there is a great difference between them. First Corinthians opens in its first chapter by saying that Christ is both theirs and ours (v. 2) and that God has called us into the fellowship of this Christ (v. 9). He is the power of God and the wisdom of God (v. 24). Christ is our righteousness for the past, our sanctification for the present, and our redemption for the future (v. 30). These points concerning Christ are presented mostly in a doctrinal way. But 2 Corinthians opens in a different way. In its first chapter Paul spoke of how he suffered in tribulation and had been comforted by God (vv. 3-6). This qualified him to comfort others. Because he had experienced the comfort of Christ through much affliction, he had this comfort with which he could comfort others.

In verses 8 and 9 Paul said, "For we do not want you to be ignorant, brothers, of our affliction which befell us in Asia, that we were excessively burdened, beyond our power, so that we despaired even of living. Indeed we ourselves had the response of death in ourselves, that we should not base our confidence on ourselves but on God, who raises the dead."

Paul and his co-workers were pressed down beyond their strength. They had the response, the sentence, of death in themselves. To their consideration, they had to die. This led them to put their trust not in themselves but in God who raises the dead. Second Corinthians shows us how the ministry is produced. It is not produced by teaching or education. It is produced through all kinds of suffering.

In chapter four Paul said that he and his co-workers were troubled in every way (vv. 8-9). They were perplexed and cast down. Paul said that they were always being put to death and that in their body they bore the putting to death of Jesus (vv. 10-11). Through such sufferings the ministry is produced. A gift is produced quickly, but a ministry takes time to be produced. To gain a gift is easy. Balaam's donkey suddenly spoke a human language. That was a real gift obtained easily. But if we are going to have a ministry, it is not so easy. A ministry is produced in a person by his experience of the riches of Christ through sufferings.

An apple tree does not come into being overnight. The apples produced by the apple tree come from the growth in life, and the growth in life is experienced through sufferings. I would encourage all of us to pray-read *Hymns*, #635. This hymn tells us how the grapevine produces grapes through sufferings. That producing of the grapevine is its ministry. It is not a gift, but a ministry. A gift is some ability, some talent, you can get overnight, but a ministry is a lifelong matter.

I do not want to disappoint or discourage the young people, but I must say that with the young ones it is hard to have a ministry. We cannot expect a young sprout to bring forth fruit. To bring forth fruit a person needs maturity, and the maturity comes into being through sufferings. We need the young ones in the church life, but we need the mature ones even more. We need those who have some ministry which comes into being through all kinds of sufferings. This is not a teaching gift, not a speaking gift, but a life-producing ministry.

Second Corinthians 4 speaks of how the outer man has to be consumed, broken, and reduced all the time (v. 16). The outer man cannot be fully reduced in a short time. Soon after

I was saved by the Lord in 1925, I thought that if I could pray much for one or two years, I would become very spiritual. Now, many years later, my feeling is that there is still too much of the oldness of the outer man with me. We all need to enter into the full sonship. We have the foretaste for our enjoyment today, and we are waiting for the full sonship, which is the redemption of our body (Rom. 8:23). To have our old man decreased, reduced, and consumed is a slow process.

The young people have many dreams of being somebody in the spiritual realm. One young person expected to be a great evangelist, but instead he became a big backslider. I love the young people, but we need to realize that they are not so trustworthy because they are in their dreams. They need the experiences of Christ through sufferings.

In 2 Corinthians the apostle Paul did not tell us how much he could do or what kind of gift he had. When he commended himself as a minister of Christ, he did not say that he had the biggest gift or that he was a great speaker, preacher, or Bible expositor. Instead, in chapter eleven he commended himself as a minister of Christ by speaking of his sufferings in following the Lord (vv. 16-33). He even said that five times under the hands of the Jews he received forty stripes less one (v. 24). I do not believe that we would write such a letter to the saints. We would want to speak only about the wonderful aspects of Christ, not about the beatings we suffered. Paul even mentioned the sufferings and perils he experienced in his journeys. He spoke of being in dangers among false brothers (v. 26).

We may wonder why the Lord would allow such a great servant of His to suffer so much. This is because the ministry is produced through sufferings. I hope that the Lord comes back soon, but it may be that He will delay His coming just because of us. We may say that we love the Lord and that the Lord will bless us. Surely He will bless us, but what do we mean when we say this? Our dictionary is different from the Lord's dictionary. The Lord does desire to bless us, but His blessing us is according to the meaning in His heavenly dictionary. Without the sufferings, we cannot experience the Lord as our blessing in a rich way. The chorus of *Hymns*, #626 says, "Each blow I suffer / Is true gain to me. / In the place of what Thou takest / Thou dost give Thyself to me." Every blow takes away something of ourselves and brings in something of the Lord. We should like this kind of trade. He takes away a part of our old man and gives back to us something of Himself.

Many of you young brothers and sisters love the Lord, but be assured that the way you are taking is the way of suffering. Since you love the Lord so much, you are on the way of sufferings all the time. Praise the Lord for the enjoyment of Christ that comes through the sufferings. Without the sufferings, it is hard to have the rich enjoyment of Christ. You can have only a superficial enjoyment. The deep enjoyment of Christ comes through suffering. I cannot tell you what kind of sufferings you will have, but the Lord knows. Step by step and year after year, He knows what you need. He knows what kind of suffering is needed to form a ministry in you.

In 2 Corinthians 6:8 Paul said that he commended himself as a minister of God not only through a good report but also through an evil report. The good report comes from the believers and those who receive the truth preached and taught by the apostles. The evil report comes from the opposers and persecutors. With the apostle Paul there were the evil reports, and if we are following the Lord in an absolute way, our experience will be the same. The evil reports are a real suffering. Paul said that his commendation was "through glory and dishonor, through evil report and good report; as deceivers and yet true" (v. 8). Glory is from God and those who love Him; dishonor is from the devil and those who follow him. Paul was a deceiver in the eyes of the Judaizers and the people of other religions and philosophies, but true in the eyes of those who loved the truth of God.

In verse 9 Paul said, "As unknown and yet well known; as dying and yet behold we live; as being disciplined and yet not being put to death." The apostles were unknown in the sense of not displaying themselves, but well known in the sense of witnessing to the truth of God. It is the same with us today. On the one hand, the apostles were dying in suffering persecutions, but on the other hand, they were living in the Lord's resurrection. Furthermore, they were being disciplined in the opposers' superficial realization. No doubt, the opposers said that Paul must have done something wrong toward God, so God was chastening him. But actually Paul was living in the sovereign care of the Lord.

During the Second World War, I was imprisoned in China by the invading Japanese army, and during that time I experienced the Lord in a special and rich way. Since you are in the hand of the Lord, you have to be prepared for sufferings. These sufferings produce the ministry. In the early part of my ministry, when I heard the evil reports and the false accusations, I was unhappy. But today when I hear these things, I am happy. Today I can thank the Lord for my imprisonment and for all the opposition and evil reports.

In verse 10 Paul said, "As made sorrowful yet always rejoicing; as poor yet enriching many; as having nothing and yet possessing all things." This describes the way of the Lord's servants, the way of those who love the Lord's way. It is through this way of suffering that a ministry will be produced with you so that you can really minister Christ to others as life. Second Corinthians 11 shows us that a minister of Christ is always passing through sufferings. We should not expect that we will not have any sufferings. This is wrong. Never be surprised when some suffering comes to you. You have to be ready. Suffering brings you the blessing, and produces a ministry for you.

Paul spoke of the sufferings in his surroundings, his circumstances, and his environment. Then when he came to chapter twelve he spoke of a thorn in his flesh, which refers to a very subjective, physical suffering in his body. In 2 Corinthians we do not see healings. Instead, we see a thorn. Paul entreated the Lord three times to remove this thorn. This was not an ordinary prayer. The Lord answered by saying that He would not take away this thorn. He would leave the thorn with Paul so that Paul could experience how sufficient the Lord's grace is and how perfect His power is in our weakness (vv. 7-9).

The apostle Paul was used by the Lord to heal others, but he could not get his physical problem healed. The Lord denied his request and told him that He would leave the thorn with him so that he might experience the Lord's sufficient grace and realize His perfect power. It was through these kinds of sufferings that Paul could have such a wonderful ministry. Paul did not consider himself to be a preacher or an expositor but a minister of Christ, dispensing Christ as life to others. The ministry is produced through sufferings and even kept through sufferings.

THE MINISTRY OF LIFE
FOR THE BUILDING UP OF THE CHURCH

Throughout its history the church has always been divided by gifts. But it can never be divided by the ministry. If we focus our attention on the gifts, we will be divided within a short time. But if we forget about the gifts and pay our full attention to the ministry of life, we will always be kept in oneness. This is why we stress again and again that the gifts cannot build up a local church, but the ministry can.

If you are a Christian worker and you are always trying to argue with others, this proves that you merely have a gift. People with the ministry of life will never argue. Argument goes along with gifts and doctrinal teachings. If we pay our attention to gifts and teachings, we will argue. But if we focus our attention on the ministry of life, we will not have anything to argue about. Gifts and teachings with doctrinal debates and arguments tear down the local church. The local church can be built up only by the ministry of life. Some may not like noisy meetings, whereas others do. We should not debate about this. What we need is the life of Christ, not a certain kind of meeting. The ministry of life does not come out of the doctrinal study and teaching of the Bible. It comes out of sufferings. If you are really in the hand of the Lord, the Lord will form a ministry with you through all kinds of sufferings.

It is so strange and wonderful that there is nothing mentioned about the gifts in 2 Corinthians. Instead there is a list of Paul's sufferings in chapter one, chapter four, chapter six, and chapter eleven. Then in chapter twelve he told us of such a subjective suffering—a thorn in the flesh. He asked the

Lord particularly to take this away, but the Lord refused. There would be no miracle, no divine healing. Instead, there would be suffering. Through the suffering, Paul experienced the Lord as the sufficient grace, which was the perfect power in his weakness. Eventually, Paul learned to say, "I will rather boast in my weaknesses" (12:9). He also said, "I am well pleased in weaknesses, in insults, in necessities, in persecutions and distresses, on behalf of Christ; for when I am weak, then I am powerful" (v. 10). This is the way to have the growth in life so that a ministry might be produced for the building up of the Body of Christ.

What is needed for the building up of a local church is the ministry of life, not the gifts. In order to illustrate this point, I would like to tell a story about Brother Watchman Nee and an elder sister by the name of Miss Barber, who helped him very much. As a young man, Brother Nee always admired good speakers. When he and Miss Barber went to hear a few speakers, Brother Nee told her how wonderful they were. But Miss Barber would say, "That is just doctrine with human eloquence. There is no life there." In other words, there was no ministry with these ones.

Brother Nee told me this at the beginning of my service in the Lord because he was trying to help me to know the difference between a ministry and a gift, that is, between the utterance of something of life and human eloquence. A person may be born with the gift of eloquence, but his speaking may be merely sounding brass. It is nice for listening, but there is no content of Christ as life. Another may be awkward in his speech, but you realize that there is something weighty with what he speaks because he has the ministry of life. This can come only out of the sufferings. The building up of the church needs this ministry of life. We all need to continue in the growth in life that we may have more ministries among us for the building up of the church.

Truth = gospel The more we preach, the more we're
Constituted. Much of my learning came from teaching
Truth - Highest gospel - man cannot be justified by the
works of law. When we believe in God, God declares righteous
We are justed out of faith in Christ. Faith is spontaneous
Faith in our appreciation is our faith as believing
Believing is _Echo_ is our believing. When we speak
the Word of Christ cause them to believe. We need to
treasure When we believe we are one
Acts 13:38, 1 COR 1:30 When God put us into Christ
God sees us in Christ. The way we're justified
Let them know as soon as righteous.
Romans We believe in resurr. Christ became
all incl LGS. 11 times gospel Actually entire
Book of Romans is gospel of God.
1. Wrath of God 2. Incarnation. _Spirit_ 30 times
4 Station Rom 1-4 Justification
          5-8 Sanct
          9-12 Body of Christ must be part of
          13-16 Local churches gospel

filled w/ God. created in God's image
corp. being. Let _them_ w/ love, joy, trust, humility
Society that is we have found heavenly
no competition, taking leading honoring one
another. Tell them rejoice & weep
enter into your suffering. We are all one body.
Paul's gospel is gospel of _sonship_
We're told Eph 1:5 predestinated unto sonship
God's predestination, motivated.
from God's please - He love the son
We need to preach speak the high gospel
present An hour is coming
Many reg. believers will be conformed as
sons of God. When we arrive in every way
To these overcoming believers, in whom
I found my delight.

Not only know, but proclaim this gospel.
became subjective. Make Paul's gospel my gospel.
separated to the gospel of God. M. Luther - justification
faithful to speak. <u>Deification by life</u>
Bro. 1:14 I am debtor to Jews, we need
much truth. We are indebted to human beings.
Preaching is paying back debt to all the human
beings both believer + unbeliever.
my gospel, so we'll be faithful.
We'll pay back obligation, satisfy God's
desire. Sanctify by grace.
In this way we'll carry out God's goal +
man's destiny.

ABOUT THE AUTHOR

Witness Lee was born in 1905 in northern China and raised in a Christian family. At age 19 he was fully captured for Christ and immediately consecrated himself to preach the gospel for the rest of his life. Early in his service, he met Watchman Nee, a renowned preacher, teacher, and writer. Witness Lee labored together with Watchman Nee under his direction. In 1934 Watchman Nee entrusted Witness Lee with the responsibility for his publication operation, called the Shanghai Gospel Bookroom.

Prior to the Communist takeover in 1949, Witness Lee was sent by Watchman Nee and his other co-workers to Taiwan to insure that the things delivered to them by the Lord would not be lost. Watchman Nee instructed Witness Lee to continue the former's publishing operation abroad as the Taiwan Gospel Bookroom, which has been publicly recognized as the publisher of Watchman Nee's works outside China. Witness Lee's work in Taiwan manifested the Lord's abundant blessing. From a mere 350 believers, newly fled from the mainland, the churches in Taiwan grew to 20,000 in five years.

In 1962 Witness Lee felt led of the Lord to come to the United States, settling in California. During his 35 years of service in the U.S., he ministered in weekly meetings and weekend conferences, delivering several thousand spoken messages. Much of his speaking has since been published as over 400 titles. Many of these have been translated into over fourteen languages. He gave his last public conference in February 1997 at the age of 91.

He leaves behind a prolific presentation of the truth in the Bible. His major work, *Life-study of the Bible*, comprises over 25,000 pages of commentary on every book of the Bible from the perspective of the believers' enjoyment and experience of God's divine life in Christ through the Holy Spirit. Witness Lee was the chief editor of a new translation of the New Testament into Chinese called the Recovery Version and directed the translation of the same into English. The Recovery Version also appears in a number of other languages. He provided an extensive body of footnotes, outlines, and spiritual cross references. A radio broadcast of his messages can be heard on Christian radio stations in the United States. In 1965 Witness Lee founded Living Stream Ministry, a non-profit corporation, located in Anaheim, California, which officially presents his and Watchman Nee's ministry.

Witness Lee's ministry emphasizes the experience of Christ as life and the practical oneness of the believers as the Body of Christ. Stressing the importance of attending to both these matters, he led the churches under his care to grow in Christian life and function. He was unbending in his conviction that God's goal is not narrow sectarianism but the Body of Christ. In time, believers began to meet simply as the church in their localities in response to this conviction. In recent years a number of new churches have been raised up in Russia and in many eastern European countries.

OTHER BOOKS PUBLISHED BY
Living Stream Ministry

Titles by Witness Lee:

Abraham—Called by God	0-7363-0359-6
The Experience of Life	0-87083-417-7
The Knowledge of Life	0-87083-419-3
The Tree of Life	0-87083-300-6
The Economy of God	0-87083-415-0
The Divine Economy	0-87083-268-9
God's New Testament Economy	0-87083-199-2
The World Situation and God's Move	0-87083-092-9
Christ vs. Religion	0-87083-010-4
The All-inclusive Christ	0-87083-020-1
Gospel Outlines	0-87083-039-2
Character	0-87083-322-7
The Secret of Experiencing Christ	0-87083-227-1
The Life and Way for the Practice of the Church Life	0-87083-785-0
The Basic Revelation in the Holy Scriptures	0-87083-105-4
The Crucial Revelation of Life in the Scriptures	0-87083-372-3
The Spirit with Our Spirit	0-87083-798-2
Christ as the Reality	0-87083-047-3
The Central Line of the Divine Revelation	0-87083-960-8
The Full Knowledge of the Word of God	0-87083-289-1
Watchman Nee—A Seer of the Divine Revelation ...	0-87083-625-0

Titles by Watchman Nee:

How to Study the Bible	0-7363-0407-X
God's Overcomers	0-7363-0433-9
The New Covenant	0-7363-0088-0
The Spiritual Man 3 volumes	0-7363-0269-7
Authority and Submission	0-7363-0185-2
The Overcoming Life	1-57593-817-0
The Glorious Church	0-87083-745-1
The Prayer Ministry of the Church	0-87083-860-1
The Breaking of the Outer Man and the Release ...	1-57593-955-X
The Mystery of Christ	1-57593-954-1
The God of Abraham, Isaac, and Jacob	0-87083-932-2
The Song of Songs	0-87083-872-5
The Gospel of God 2 volumes	1-57593-953-3
The Normal Christian Church Life	0-87083-027-9
The Character of the Lord's Worker	1-57593-322-5
The Normal Christian Faith	0-87083-748-6
Watchman Nee's Testimony	0-87083-051-1

Available at
Christian bookstores, or contact Living Stream Ministry
2431 W. La Palma Ave. • Anaheim, CA 92801
1-800-549-5164 • www.livingstream.com